Black & White

politically incorrect essays

*on politics, culture, science,
religion, energy, and environment*

David Deming

DEDICATION

This book is dedicated to all the skeptics and heretics. It is dedicated to Pyrrho, Socrates, and Jesus Christ. To Roger Bacon, Martin Luther, Paracelsus, and Peter Ramus. I make my dedication to Galileo, and all the victims of narrow-minded intellectual bigotry and intolerance. It is the unreasonable men who are the guiding lights of the human race. For knowledge begins with skepticism and ends with conceit.

CONTENTS

PREFACE

This book contains fifty short essays written between 1992 and 2011. Most of these were composed between 2003 and 2011. I have made some minor editorial changes to remove anachronisms and insert dates where necessary. These essays are polemics, not scholarly works. They are meant to inform, but consist primarily of opinion. The diverse range of topics mirrors my own wide range of interests. The title of the book is a play on words. The phrase "black and white" refers not only to the format of the text, but also metaphorically to the fact that I have written forthrightly without consideration for cultural conventions or what other people might deem to be politically correct.

.

1 THE PETROLEUM AGE IS JUST BEGINNING

It is hard to imagine how our grandparents and great-grandparents lived at the end of the nineteenth century. The United States was still largely a rural society, and the amenities we take for granted today were unknown then. Most people lived on farms. Few Americans had running water, bathtubs, hot water, or flush toilets. Central heating, electricity, and telephones were rare. There were no antibiotics. Infant mortality was high, and life expectancy was thirty years lower than it is today. For most people, educational opportunities were very limited. In 1890, only 5 percent of the eligible population attended high school.

In the year 1900, there were only about 8,000 automobiles in the entire country. Horseless carriages, like yachts, were a toy for the rich to enjoy. People knew there would never be enough gasoline to power a nation of automobiles because the output of the Pennsylvanian oil fields had been declining for years.

The seminal event that transformed the United States into an industrial and technological powerhouse occurred on the morning of January 10, 1901, near Beaumont, Texas. A wildcat oil well on a location named Spindletop erupted into a geyser a hundred feet high. It was the greatest oil well ever seen in the United States.

Over the next year, production from the Spindletop well equaled the production of 37,000 typical oil wells in the eastern U.S. Overnight, the price of oil dropped to three cents a barrel, recovering to 83 cents a barrel two and half years later. The cheap energy provided by abundant oil allowed the U.S. to transform itself from a rural, agrarian country into an urban, industrialized nation. Along the way, the prosperity of our society increased manyfold.

Petroleum continues to be the lifeblood of our technological civilization. Our entire way of life depends on the energy that is provided by the oil industry. Oil and natural gas are by far the most important energy sources for the world. Their combustion also generates far less pollution than the third most-relied-upon energy source, coal.

The best news is that the age of petroleum has only just begun. For more than eighty years, geological estimates of the world's endowment of oil have risen faster than humanity can pump it out of the ground. In 1920, the US Geological Survey estimated that the total amount of oil remaining in the world amounted to only 20 billion barrels. By the year 2000, the estimate had grown to 3000 billion barrels. In recent years, increases in the price of oil have caused estimates of the size of the ultimate resource to be repeatedly revised upward. In 2005, the International Energy Agency estimated that 5500 billion barrels of oil could be eventually recovered from the Earths crust.

Geologists are continually forced to revise their estimates upward, because every year technological advances make it possible to draw upon petroleum resources whose extraction were once unthinkable. We can now drill wells up to 30,000 feet deep. The amount of oil that can be recovered from a single well has been enhanced by a technology that allows multiple horizontal shafts to be branched off from one vertical borehole. The ability to drill offshore in water depths of up to 9,000 feet has opened up the vast petroleum resources of the world's submerged continental margins.

The world also contains immense amounts of unconventional oil resources that we have not yet begun to tap. For example, tar sands found in Canada and South America contain 600 billion barrels of oil, enough to supply the U.S. with 84 years of oil at the current consumption rate. Worldwide, the amount of oil that can be extracted from oil shales could be as large as 14,000 billion barrels--enough to supply the world for 500 years.

Oil is by far the cheapest, most abundant, and cleanest source of energy we have. Nearly every advantage we enjoy today can be traced back to the energy provided by the petroleum industry. Yet the men and women who make our civilization possible are too often treated as pariahs who are damaging the environment. This is a shame. The environmental impacts of petroleum exploration and production are virtually negligible in comparison to the benefits they provide.

All of us want to preserve and protect the natural environment, but much of the modern environmental movement is based upon the myth of a primitive harmony with nature that has never existed. Life without oil and technology is a life that is short, dark, and impoverished. Let us give thanks that we have been lifted out of darkness and poverty.

2 THE OIL PRICE BUBBLE

The retail price of gasoline in the US has been over $2 a gallon since March of 2005, and peaked over $3 in September of 2005. Fortunately, geological evidence indicates that current oil prices are unsustainable. Barring any significant geopolitical disruption, that means cheaper prices at the pump for the American consumer.

All geologists agree that the total amount of petroleum in the earth's crust is fixed and must decrease with continued production. Over the last 150 years, almost exactly a trillion barrels of oil has been withdrawn. As the world's endowment of oil is slowly drawn down, it is a virtual certainty that eventually the price will increase to the point that the cost of extraction will exceed the value of energy obtained.

Recent increases in the cost of crude oil have given rise to renewed speculation that world oil production is about to peak. At the beginning of 2004, oil was $34 per barrel, but the price briefly reached $70 in late August of 2005. A price of about $60 in 2006 is high by any historical standard.

However, the surge in oil prices we have seen in recent years is not a sign the world is beginning to run out of oil. On the contrary, it is a positive indicator of increased economic activity. High prices will encourage development of more of the world's enormous petroleum reserves.

In 2000, the US Geological Survey estimated that the amount of conventional oil that would ultimately be withdrawn from the earth's crust was three trillion barrels. One-third of this has already been produced. Another third consists of petroleum reserves that have been identified and can be extracted using current technology. The last trillion barrels remains to be discovered.

One way to determine if the world is beginning to run out of oil is to look at the ratio of petroleum reserves to annual production. In the 1960s, the average ratio of world petroleum reserves to production was 35. During the energy crises of the 1970s, the ratio decreased to 32. In the 1980s, it increased to 37. During the 1990s, the ratio of reserves to annual production rose to 45. In 2010, the ratio of world oil reserves to annual production was 56, a record high.

If the world were beginning to run out of oil, our technological ability to generate new petroleum reserves through exploration and technology would begin to be outstripped by consumption. The ratio of reserves to production would start to decrease. Yet for the last 50 years, the trend is one of increasing, rather than decreasing, supply.

So, why has the price of oil increased so dramatically in recent years? From 2002 through 2004, demand for oil increased at an average annual rate of 3.7%. This is more than triple the rate of increase from 1990 through 2000, which averaged an anemic 1.1%. Low demand during the 1990s, combined with surging reserves, caused oil prices to bottom out near $10 a barrel in December 1998. In February 1999, the average retail price of gasoline in the US was 90 cents a gallon. As a result, oil companies were reluctant to bring more reserves into production.

The largest mistake we could make at this time would be to start to move away from petroleum, a proven and economic energy source, to more speculative and expensive sources. Not only do we have a trillion barrels of conventional oil in reserve, there are huge amounts of unconventional oil resources awaiting development. The International Energy Administration recently estimated that at a price of $60 a barrel or more, it will be economic to recover at least another two trillion barrels of petroleum from tar sands and oil shales.

The world will eventually leave the age of oil, but there is no geologic reason for this to happen until near the end of the twenty-first century.

.

3 OIL FUELS HUMAN PROGRESS

In ancient times, the rate of human progress was so slow as to be indiscernible. People lived and died as their ancestors had done. Their outlook was pessimistic. In the second century AD, Roman Emperor Marcus Aurelius wrote that anyone who had lived for forty years had seen "all that is past and future."

Human beings did not begin to develop a more optimistic outlook until the sixteenth century when Francis Bacon recognized that "by far the greatest obstacle to the progress of science is that men despair and think things impossible." The principle of progress was developed and embraced by eighteenth-century Enlightenment philosophers. In 1768, chemist Joseph Priestley predicted "whatever was the beginning of this world, the end will be glorious and paradisaical."

Priestley's prediction was fully realized in the Industrial Revolution, a transformation that continues to sweep through the world today. In the last 200 years, the productive capacity of the American worker has increased by a factor of 36. By 1970, the diseases of diphtheria, polio, malaria, smallpox, typhoid fever, and whooping cough had virtually disappeared from the US. Life expectancies doubled. Since 1850, the length of the average work week in America has decreased from 66 to 35 hours. In 1997, the United Nations noted that world poverty had fallen more in the last 50 years than in the previous 500.

As our prosperity is increasing, the quality of our environment is improving. Since 1970, air pollution in the US has declined by 63 percent, even while our energy use increased by 40 percent. Over the same period of time, water pollution in the US declined significantly.

Human progress depends on abundant and inexpensive energy from fossil fuels, including petroleum. Fossil fuels provide 85 percent of the world's energy, and oil is the largest single source. Since the large-scale exploitation of petroleum resources began in the nineteenth century, the world has consumed a trillion barrels of oil. But the resource is far from exhausted. In the last ten years, geological estimates of the size of the ultimate petroleum resource have grown from about 2.5 trillion barrels to 5.5 trillion barrels. Human beings are discovering new oil resources at a rate ten times faster than we are consuming the resource.

There is at least enough oil to provide for the world's energy needs to the end of this century. Ultimately however, petroleum is a finite resource that will be unable to power human civilization indefinitely. No technology is sustainable, all are bridges to greater human achievement. But at the present time all alternatives to fossil fuels have severe deficiencies. These limitations are not due to a lack of political will, but the laws of chemistry and physics.

Finding new energy sources will require decades of research and development. The technologies of the future are being developed today at the University of Oklahoma. But impoverished societies cannot fund scientific research or afford clean environments. To create the future, we need to continue the development and utilization of fossil fuels. Indeed, much of the funding for education and research at OU comes directly from the energy industry.

Human progress is sustainable only if we maintain an optimistic attitude, continue to increase our prosperity and energy utilization, and invest in education and research. The greatest danger to human civilization today is not environmental degradation, but a return to the ancient plague of pessimism.

4 NATURAL GAS: FUEL OF THE FUTURE

Historically, Oklahoma has been noted for its oil production. But the most important energy resource in Oklahoma today is natural gas, or methane. Gas is an abundant, inexpensive, and environmentally-friendly energy source. Methane is also a flexible and reliable power source. In addition to heating homes, powering industry, and generating electricity, it can be used in vehicles for transportation. Oklahoma's clean-burning natural gas is the fuel of the future, and one solution to America's current energy crisis.

In comparison to other energy sources, natural gas has some marked advantages. Coal is inexpensive and abundant, but burning coal releases pollutants such as nitrous oxides, sulfur, particulate matter, and the toxic metals mercury and arsenic. Acid rain from coal combustion can damage both wildlife and trees. Coal mining is dangerous, and streams can be polluted by the acid runoff from coal mine tailings.

Wind and solar power are good things that ought to be developed in Oklahoma, but they have a limited capacity to add to the energy mix. Both wind and solar power are expensive, intermittent, and neither can be used directly for transportation. We need biofuel research, but it is not clear at the present time if ethanol delivers more energy than is used in its production. Hydrogen is not a power source, but an energy carrier. Nuclear power is a proven means of generating electricity, but cannot be used for transportation. Nuclear is also politically contentious, generates radioactive waste, and has the potential to facilitate weapons proliferation.

Everyone is in favor of energy conservation and efficiency. But a consensus is now developing that we can't grow our economy through conservation, or rely solely upon nascent renewable-energy technologies that have serious limitations. Fossil fuels are the bridge to the future, and natural gas is the most reliable, abundant and environmentally benign energy source available.

The good news is that recent technological innovations have opened up vast new domestic gas resources. There is no danger that we are going to run out of methane at any time in the foreseeable future, nor do we have to rely upon imports from the Middle East. Improvements in hydraulic fracturing and horizontal drilling techniques have made it possible to produce significant quantities of gas from new sources right here in the conterminous US. The US currently consumes about 22 trillion cubic feet (TCF) of gas each year, of which less than 20 percent is imported from Canada and Mexico. At this consumption rate, domestic resources are sufficient to meet our energy needs for more than a hundred years.

In recent years, Oklahoma's independent energy companies have made massive investments in exploration, production, and transportation infrastructure. These investments insure that American prosperity based on environmentally friendly and reliable energy will continue far into the distant future. Oklahoma's own natural gas is the best choice to meet American energy needs for the coming century.

5 LOTS OF OIL LEFT

For more than a hundred years, people have been claiming that the world is running out of oil. But there is no factual support for the claim that the world's petroleum resources are nearing exhaustion. The world has enough oil left to supply demand through the end of this century.

In 1954, the year I was born, the world had 158 billion barrels of petroleum in reserve, about 32 times the annual production rate of 5 billion barrels. But at the end of 2010, the world's oil reserves were 1,470 billion barrels, or about 56 times annual world production.

Since the nineteenth century, cumulative world oil production has amounted to a little more than a trillion barrels. But the geological endowment of conventional oil alone may be as large as 10 trillion barrels. Aided by advances in technology, petroleum companies continue to find and develop significant new deposits.

In the first six months of 2009, oil companies worldwide discovered 10 billion barrels of new petroleum accumulations. There is also a lot of oil left in the US. The outer continental shelves of the US are estimated to hold 86 billion barrels of petroleum. In September of 2009, BP discovered a new deepwater field in the Gulf of Mexico that promises to produce 4 to 6 billion barrels.

The Williston Basin in Montana and North Dakota contains nearly 4 billion barrels of oil that has yet to be discovered and produced. Oil has been produced from the Williston Basin since the 1920s. But the introduction of horizontal drilling and hydrofracturing have made it possible to exploit resources heretofore unreachable. Among the leaders in using the new technologies is Oklahoma's own Continental Resources.

North America contains huge unconventional petroleum resources in the form of tar sands and oil shale. The western US alone is capable of producing at least 2 trillion barrels of petroleum from oil shale. At a current US annual consumption rate of 7 billion barrels, that represents a 286-year supply of oil, none of which would be imported. The value of this resource is $120 trillion, ten times the size of the US national debt.

We should follow Canada's example. Starting in the 1960s, Canada began to aggressively develop its tar sand resources. As a result, Canadian production is now more than a million barrels per day, and its oil reserves are the second-largest in the world.

Oil is the lifeblood of our industrial economy. The US economy will remain stagnant and depressed until we begin to aggressively develop our native energy resources. We have the technology to produce petroleum from oil shale in a manner that is efficient, economic, and environmentally friendly. What's stopping us is ignorance and bad public policy.

Our energy policies today are not being determined by common sense, science, or the needs of the American people, but by a radical environmental ideology that promises nothing less than a return to the Stone Age. Our problems with energy don't originate in geology, but in knowledge and politics.

6 FOSSIL FUELS BENEFIT HUMANITY

I have never heard a more ignorant statement than the claim that we are "addicted" to oil. One might as well complain that the human race is "addicted" to prosperity, because oil and other fossil fuels are largely responsible for ending endemic poverty. Over the past two hundred years, the widespread use of fossil fuels has produced unprecedented advances in nearly every aspect of human welfare.

Most people today have no idea of how hard life was before the Industrial Revolution. At the beginning of the nineteenth century, life expectancy at birth for people living in the most advanced areas of the world was only about 25 years, less than one-third the current US life expectancy of 78 years. Infant mortality was fifty percent and infectious diseases were rampant.

Conditions only began to improve after James Watt made the steam engine an efficient and portable source of power. Steam engines driven by burning coal facilitated the mass production of commodities in factories. Coal also provided a means to efficiently transport goods long distances at low cost by powering railroad locomotives and ships.

In the twentieth century oil began to replace coal, and the steam engine was superseded by the internal combustion engine. Automobiles and airplanes reduced travel times from months or weeks to hours. The introduction of gasoline-powered tractors dramatically increased farm production. In the year 1800, 75 percent of Americans farmed. But today's farmers are so productive that 2 percent of our population produces enough food to feed everyone.

The prosperity provided by fossil fuels funds education, the arts, and scientific research. During the twentieth century, the number of adolescents in the US enrolled in high school increased from 6 to 94 percent, and the number of adults graduating from college increased from 3 to 25 percent. By

1970, medical science had virtually eradicated the diseases of diptheria, polio, malaria, smallpox, typhoid fever, and whooping cough from the US.

People living today are not only much more prosperous than their ancestors, they also have more leisure time. Between 1850 and 2000, the productivity of the US worker increased by a factor of 10, while the length of the work week decreased from 66 to 35 hours.

In the last hundred years American households acquired the flush toilet, telephone, refrigerator, electric light, radio, television, vacuum cleaner, washing machine, microwave oven, and personal computer. All of these devices are powered by electricity produced almost entirely by burning fossil fuels.

The quality of our natural environment is also improving in some significant ways. Since 1970, aggregate emissions of the six major air pollutants tracked by the EPA have decreased by 63 percent, even while US population rose 50 percent and energy consumption increased by 40 percent.

Neither are we in any imminent danger of depleting our supplies of fossil fuels. Petroleum reserves are at an all-time high. Oil reserves are technically defined as identified resources that can be economically extracted using current technology. In the year I was born, 1954, the world's annual consumption of petroleum was 5 billion barrels with 158 billion barrels, a 32 year supply, in reserve. In 2010, world oil consumption was 26 billion barrels with 1470 billion barrels in reserve. In terms of annual consumption, we have 56 years of oil in reserve. World oil reserves are now significantly higher than they were 1954, whether measured in absolute volume or in terms of years of supply.

Petroleum reserves are a fraction of the total resource. In the year 2000, the U.S. Geological Survey estimated that the world's ultimate recoverable oil resources amounted to 3 trillion barrels. But price increases and technological advances in recent years have caused resource estimates to soar. In 2003, the International Energy Administration estimated that at prices of $70. a barrel or greater, the world resource is 5.5 trillion barrels.

North America contains huge unconventional petroleum resources in the form of tar sands and oil shale. Starting in the 1960s, Canada began to aggressively develop its tar sand resources. As a result, Canadian production is now more than a million barrels per day, and its oil reserves are the third-largest in the world. Canada is also the leading supplier of petroleum to the US.

The western US alone is capable of producing at least 2 trillion barrels of petroleum from oil shale. At a current US annual consumption rate of 7 billion barrels, this represents a 286-year supply of oil, none of which would be imported. At $100. a barrel, the value of this resource is $200 trillion, fourteen times the size of the US national debt. If we had followed Canada's example we would not be in an economic recession and we would not be paying $4. a gallon for gasoline.

Coal, oil, and natural gas are the most inexpensive, abundant, and reliable sources of energy. These three fossil fuels supply 80 percent of the world's energy and are projected to remain the world's primary energy sources for the next several decades. The energy industries that produce and supply fossil fuels are the greatest benefactors of humanity in all history.

7 THE PIPELINE CONTROVERSY IS MANUFACTURED

There is a supposed controversy concerning the construction of a pipeline to bring oil from Canada to the United States. Opposition to the Keystone XL Pipeline has become a great moral cause. Hollywood actress Daryl Hannah was recently arrested while protesting the pipeline at the White House. Hannah, a vegetarian and environmental activist, has a history of demonstrating her moral superiority by arranging to have herself arrested for environmental causes. Her qualifications in the field of energy include playing movie roles such as a mermaid, a stripper, and a cavewoman.

The pipeline controversy is manufactured. The successful completion of this pipeline will increase the supply of oil coming into the US and thereby decrease its price and the price of refined products such as gasoline. Is there anyone who thinks gasoline is too cheap? Expensive energy is a burden on the economy and a cause of high unemployment. Is there anyone who wants fewer jobs and more unemployment?

It is a startling moral inversion for a Hollywood movie actress to protest petroleum. Oklahoma petroleum companies put people to work. They produce wealth and prosperity for everyone, and have selflessly donated tens of million of dollars to institutions like hospitals and universities that promote human welfare and the progress of civilization. In contrast, Daryl Hannah entertains people, in part by taking off her clothes. From where does this woman derive her moral authority?

The pipeline is controversial exclusively to a handful of environmental fanatics whose ignorance is exceeded only by their vanity. These people have been given attention in the media all out of proportion to their representation in the population. They have replaced the common sense conservation ethics of John Muir, Theodore Roosevelt, and Aldo Leopold by a fanatical environmentalism that is opposed to all human technology and progress.

To the extent that any controversy may exist, the controversy ought to be why the US has to import petroleum from Canada. Canada produces more petroleum than it consumes because Canadians had the foresight to develop their resources. In the 1960s, the Canadians began to develop the technology and infrastructure to produce oil from their native tar sands. Now Canada has the third largest store of oil reserves in the world. By contrast, we sit on vast undeveloped petroleum resources. The Western US alone contains two trillion barrels of petroleum in the form of oil shales. That's trillion with a "t," nearly a three-hundred year supply at current consumption rates. The technology exists to develop this vast resource and bring it economically to market at current prices. But development has been blocked by environmentalists.

At $80 a barrel, US oil shale has a value of $160 trillion, more than ten times the US national debt. Production would go a long way toward building the wealth necessary to create jobs and pay off our debt. We need to free ourselves from the shackles of radical environmentalism, go back to work, and start producing energy and wealth.

8 CUTTING THE KNOT OF GLOBAL WARMING

With the release of the new Al Gore movie, *An Inconvenient Truth*, hysteria regarding global warming has reached a fever pitch. Gore himself has gone so far as to state that a vengeful God will destroy humanity if global warming is allowed to continue. It's not the first time that people have become abandoned reason to indulge themselves in a self-righteous moral frenzy. For centuries, Europeans were obsessed with the idea that witches and evil spirits were responsible for all of the ills that beset mankind. Over a period of about 300 years, nearly 60,000 people were executed for the crime of witchcraft.

Although the Witch Mania of Medieval Europe is today viewed as the offspring of prejudice and superstition, the intelligent opinion of the day considered the existence of witches to be based upon overwhelming empirical support that was beyond question by a rational person.

Writing in 1588, Montaigne acknowledged this when he said that the "proofs and reasons" supporting the prosecution of witches "had no end." Therefore, he explained, he would cut the knot, as Alexander cut the Gordian Knot, because "'tis setting a man's conjectures at a very high price, upon them to cause a man to be roasted alive." Similarly, flushing 500 years of technological progress down the toilet is a very high price to pay for hypothetical conjectures concerning possible future climate change.

At one time, scientists were dedicated solely to the objective pursuit of truth, not the advocacy of social and political issues. In 1676, Robert Hooke wrote "I have a mind very desirous of and very ready to embrace any truth that shall be discovered though it may much thwart and contradict any opinions or notions I have formerly embraced."

But the ethic of a disinterested search for truth is foreign to most scientists working today. These individuals typically receive no education or training in philosophy or the history of science. They tend to be specialized technical workers who do not understand that when one searches only for confirming evidence it will always be found. In a word, they are ignorant; ignorant of science, ignorant of history, and ignorant of their own ignorance.

For more than a decade, both the mass media and editorial staff of major scientific journals have repressed contrarian and skeptical views regarding climate change. In 1995, a reporter for National Public Radio began his interview with me by asking me if I believed that warming was due to human activities. When I told him the evidence was inconclusive, he snorted "no one is interested in that point of view," and hung up on me.

The public has no appreciation for how distorted the information is they receive. We are told that recent years are the "warmest on record," but are left ignorant of the fact that the beginning of the instrumental record coincides with the end of the Little Ice Age, or that temperatures for much of human history were warmer.

We are informed that a computer model predicts drastic warming in the future. But we are not told that the model which predicts this warming is the most extreme of thirty such models, or that it is impossible to verify any computer model, all of which contain significant uncertainties.

We are warned that global warming will result in sea level rises, but not that warmer temperatures will have many beneficial effects, such as longer growing seasons at high latitudes. Every natural disaster that occurs, even tsunamis caused by earthquakes, is blamed on global warming. The litany of doom mongering is endless, but it is all based on either outright fraud or a dishonest and selective presentation of the facts.

So, like Montaigne, I choose to cut the knot of global warming. This rash of ignorant conceit, hysterical nonsense, and rabid demagoguery is a fanatical assault on knowledge, civilization, and human enlightenment.

9 INHOFE CORRECT ON GLOBAL WARMING

Oklahoma Senator James Inhofe has been taking a lot of heat lately for his skeptical stance on global warming. He's been called a "social dinosaur" for his failure to accept the politically-correct view. But in my opinion, Senator Inhofe is absolutely correct.

I'm a geophysicist who has conducted and published climate studies in top-rank scientific journals. My perspective on Senator Inhofe and the issue of global warming is informed not only by my knowledge of climate science, but also by my studies of the history and philosophy of science.

The media hysteria on global warming has been generated by journalists who don't understand the provisional and uncertain nature of scientific knowledge. Science changes. For years we were told that drinking coffee was bad for our health and would increase our risk for heart disease. But more recent studies have shown that not only is coffee safe for our hearts, it can decrease the risk of liver cancer and is chock full of healthy antioxidants.

I read recently that temperatures are now higher than at any time in the past 12,000 years. The fact that the thermometer wasn't invented until the year 1714, ought to give us pause when evaluating this remarkable claim. Reconstructions of past temperatures are not *measurements*, but *estimates*. These estimates are based on innumerable interpretations and uncertain assumptions, all invisible to someone who only reads the headline. Better studies--completely ignored by the major media--have shown that late twentieth-century temperatures are not anomalous or unusually warm.

It has also been claimed that in a mere fifty years mean global temperatures on Earth will be higher than they have been for the last million years. We all know that in recent years weather forecasts have become more accurate. But meteorologists can't predict what the temperature will be in 30 days. How is it that we are supposed to believe that they can reliably predict what the temperature will be in fifty years? They can't, because Earth's climate system is complex and poorly understood.

It is not surprising that some scientists today find evidence to support global warming. True believers *always* find confirming evidence. In the late 18th century, a school of geologists known as Neptunists became convinced that all of the rocks of the Earth's crust had been precipitated from water. British geologist Robert Jameson characterized the supporting evidence for Neptunism as "incontrovertible." The Neptunists were completely wrong, but able to explain away any evidence that appeared to contradict their theory. A skeptic pointed out that not all rocks could be formed by water because he had observed molten lava from a volcano cool and solidify into rock. Unperturbed, the Neptunists calmly explained that the heat of the volcano had merely melted a rock originally formed by water.

Around 1996, I became aware of how corrupt and ideologically-driven current climate research can be. A major researcher working in the area of climate change confided in me that the factual record needed to be altered so that people would become alarmed over global warming. He said "we have to get rid of the Medieval Warm Period."

The Medieval Warm Period was a time of unusually warm weather that began around 1000 AD and persisted until a cold period known as the "Little Ice Age" took hold in the 14th and 15th centuries. The warmer climate of the Medieval Warm Period was accompanied by a remarkable flowering of prosperity, knowledge, and art in Europe. But the existence of the Medieval Warm Period was an "inconvenient truth" for true believers in global warming. It needed to be erased from history so that people could become convinced that present day temperatures were truly anomalous. Unfortunately, the prostitution of science to environmental ideology is all too common.

Senator James Inhofe is not only correct in his view on global warming, but courageous to insist on truth, objectivity and sound science. Truth in science doesn't depend on human consensus or political correctness. The fact that the majority of journalists and pundits bray like sheep is meaningless. Galileo, another "social dinosaur," said "the crowd of fools who know nothing is infinite."

10 US SENATE TESTIMONY ON GLOBAL WARMING

Mr. Chairman, members of the Committee, and distinguished guests, thank you for inviting me to testify today. I am a geologist and geophysicist. I have a bachelor's degree in geology from Indiana University, and a Ph.D in geophysics from the University of Utah. My field of specialization in geophysics is temperature and heat flow. In recent years, I have turned my studies to the history and philosophy of science.

In 1995, I published a short paper in the academic journal *Science*. In that study, I reviewed how borehole temperature data recorded a warming of about one degree Celsius in North America over the last 100 to 150 years. The week the article appeared, I was contacted by a reporter for National Public Radio. He offered to interview me, but only if I would state that the warming was due to human activity. When I refused to do so, he hung up on me.

I had another interesting experience around the time my paper in *Science* was published. I received an astonishing email from a major researcher in the area of climate change. He said, "We have to get rid of the Medieval Warm Period."

The Medieval Warm Period (MWP) was a time of unusually warm weather that began around 1000 AD and persisted until a cold period known as the "Little Ice Age" took hold in the 14th century. Warmer climate brought a remarkable flowering of prosperity, knowledge, and art to Europe during the High Middle Ages.

The existence of the MWP had been recognized in the scientific literature for decades. But now it was a major embarrassment to those maintaining that the 20th century warming was truly anomalous. It had to be "gotten rid of."

In 1769, Joseph Priestley warned that scientists overly attached to a favorite hypothesis would not hesitate to "warp the whole course of nature."

In 1999, Michael Mann and his colleagues published a reconstruction of past temperature in which the MWP simply vanished. This unique estimate became known as the "hockey stick," because of the shape of the temperature graph.

Normally in science, when you have a novel result that appears to overturn previous work, you have to demonstrate why the earlier work was wrong. But the work of Mann and his colleagues was initially accepted uncritically, even though it contradicted the results of more than 100 previous studies. Other researchers have since reaffirmed that the Medieval Warm Period was both warm and global in its extent.

There is an overwhelming bias today in the media regarding the issue of global warming. In the past two years, this bias has bloomed into an irrational hysteria. Every natural disaster that occurs is now linked with global warming, no matter how tenuous or impossible the connection. As a result, the public has become vastly misinformed on this and other environmental issues.

Earth's climate system is complex and poorly understood. But we do know that throughout human history, warmer temperatures have been associated with more stable climates and increased human health and prosperity. Colder temperatures have been correlated with climatic instability, famine, and increased human mortality.

The amount of climatic warming that has taken place in the past 150 years is poorly constrained, and its cause--human or natural--is unknown. There is no sound scientific basis for predicting future climate change with any degree of certainty. If the climate does warm, it is likely to be beneficial to humanity rather than harmful. In my opinion, it would be foolish to establish national energy policy on the basis of misinformation and irrational hysteria.

11 INCONVENIENT TRUTHS

The largest single factor driving the debate on global warming is the Al Gore film *An Inconvenient Truth*. The movie has been marketed as a scientific documentary, but in fact it is an artful and deceptive propaganda film.

The claims made in *An Inconvenient Truth* are either wrong, disingenuous, or misleading at best. Gore frightens his audience by showing the breakup of the Larsen Ice Shelf on the Antarctic Peninsula. He then states that if the West Antarctic Ice Sheet were to melt it would raise sea level worldwide by twenty feet. But Gore conveniently neglects to inform us that over the last several decades, eighty to ninety percent of Antarctica has been growing colder, in direct contradiction to greenhouse theory. The main ice accumulation in Antarctica is not melting, it's getting thicker.

Gore leads his audience to believe that for the last 650,000 years of Earth's climate history, carbon dioxide has determined temperature. But it's well documented in the scientific literature that changes in temperature preceded changes in carbon dioxide. Temperature controlled carbon dioxide by regulating the release and absorption of this gas from the oceans.

An Inconvenient Truth fails to inform viewers that projections of future warming from carbon dioxide are based on computer models whose reliability and accuracy are completely unknown. As a scientist who has done computer modeling and studied geophysical inverse theory, I find it alarming that people are seriously considering restructuring our entire civilization on the basis of computer models that cannot even be tested.

Gore's claim that "zero percent" of scientists disagree on global warming is not true, and demonstrates a profound ignorance of science and the provisional nature of scientific knowledge. The former Vice President of the United States could also use a lesson on basic economics. He makes the remarkable claim that we won't damage our economy by switching from fossil fuels--which are inexpensive, reliable, and abundant--to alternative fuel sources that are expensive, unreliable, and scarce. Europe's experience demonstrates otherwise. As reported in the *Washington Post* on April 9, 2007, Europe's attempt to reduce carbon dioxide emissions has proven to be a bureaucratic nightmare, with high energy prices, unforeseen consequences, and "significant economic costs." European businesses are losing customers to Chinese competitors.

Oh yes, China. The Chinese currently have 2000 coal-fired power plants, and are proceeding to enthusiastically grow their economy by building a new plant every week. Incredibly, Al Gore says that China should get a free pass on carbon dioxide. He wants the average American to shoulder the responsibility for stopping global warming.

The package for *An Inconvenient Truth* instructs us how to accomplish this. We are supposed to alter the composition of Earth's atmosphere by switching from incandescent to fluorescent light bulbs, keeping the tires on our cars properly inflated, and planting trees. As a testament to the monumental stature of human stupidity, these recommendations are only exceeded by pop singer Sheryl Crow's recent assertion that global warming can be stopped by restricting the use of toilet paper.

On the morning of April 8, 2007, Charlotte, North Carolina, experienced a low temperature of 21 degrees Fahrenheit. It was the coldest temperature ever recorded in Charlotte for the month of April. But if you think record cold weather is going to falsify global warming, you're hopelessly naive. On April 11, 2007, a Purdue professor told the *Christian Science Monitor* that "this is what you might expect of global warming," because global warming "isn't necessarily always a warmer climate, but a more variable climate." In other words, all weather variations are evidence for global warming. I can't make this stuff up.

Global warming has long since moved from scientific hypothesis to pseudoscientific mumbo-jumbo. It is the latest and most successful in a long line of disingenuous excuses to wage war on technology, progress, and the human mind. The predatory demagogues who peddle this dangerous nonsense are enemies of the human race.

12 YEAR OF GLOBAL COOLING

According to Al Gore, global warming is a planetary emergency. It is difficult to see how this can be the case when record low temperatures are being set all over the world. In 2007, hundreds of people died, not from global warming, but from cold weather hazards.

Since the middle of the nineteenth century, the mean global temperature has increased by 0.7 °C. This slight warming is not unusual, and lies well within the range of natural variation. Carbon dioxide continues to build up in the atmosphere, but the mean planetary temperature hasn't increased significantly for nearly nine years. Antarctica is getting colder. Neither the intensity nor the frequency of hurricanes has increased. The 2007 season was the third quietest since 1966, and in 2006 not a single hurricane made landfall in the US.

South America experienced one of its coldest winters in decades. In Buenos Aires, snow fell for the first time since the year 1918. Dozens of homeless people died from exposure. In Peru, two hundred people died from the cold and thousands more became infected with respiratory diseases. Crops failed, livestock perished, and the Peruvian government declared a state of emergency. Unexpected bitter cold swept across the entire southern hemisphere in 2007. Johannesburg, South Africa, had the first significant snowfall in 26 years. Australia experienced the coldest June ever. In northeastern Australia, the city of Townsville underwent the longest period of continuously cold weather since 1941. In New Zealand, the weather turned so cold that vineyards were in danger of going out of business.

In January of 2007 $1.42 billion of California produce was lost to a devastating five-day freeze. Thousands of agricultural employees were thrown out of work. At the supermarket, citrus prices soared. In the wake of the freeze, California Governor Arnold Schwarzenegger asked President Bush to issue a disaster declaration for affected counties. A few months earlier, Schwarzenegger had enthusiastically signed the California Global Warming Solutions Act of 2006, a law designed to cool the climate. California Senator Barbara Boxer continues to push for similar legislation in the US Senate.

In April of 2007, a killing freeze destroyed 95 percent of South Carolina's peach crop, and 90 percent of North Carolina's apple harvest. At Charlotte, North Carolina, a record low temperature of 21 °F on April 8, 2007, was the coldest temperature ever recorded for the month of April, breaking a record set in 1923. On June 8, 2007, Denver recorded a new low of 31 °F. Denver's temperature records extend back to 1872.

In the fall and winter of 2007, unusually cold conditions returned to the northern hemisphere. On December 7, St. Cloud, Minnesota, set a new record low of minus 15 °F. On the same date, record low temperatures were also recorded in Pennsylvania and Ohio. The winter of 2007 was marked by extreme cold weather worldwide. On December 4, in Seoul, Korea, the temperature was a record minus 5 °C. On November 24, in Meacham, Oregon, the minimum temperature was 12 °F colder than the previous record low set in 1952. The Canadian government warned that the winter of 2007 was likely to be the coldest in 15 years.

Oklahoma, Kansas, and Missouri experienced a destructive ice storm that left at least 36 people dead and a million without electric power. People worldwide were reminded of what used to be common sense: cold temperatures are inimical to human welfare and warm weather is beneficial. Left in the dark and cold, Oklahomans rushed out to buy electric generators powered by gasoline, not solar cells. No one seemed particularly concerned about the welfare of polar bears, penguins, or walruses. Fossil fuels don't seem so awful when you're in the cold and dark.

If you think that any of the preceding facts can falsify global warming, you're hopelessly naive. Nothing creates cognitive dissonance in the mind of a true believer. In 2005, a Canadian Greenpeace representative explained "global warming can mean colder, it can mean drier, it can mean wetter." In other words, all weather variations are evidence for global warming. I can't make this stuff up. Global warming has long since passed from scientific hypothesis to the realm of pseudo-scientific mumbo-jumbo.

13 THE COMING ICE AGE

Those who ignore the geologic perspective do so at great risk. In fall of 1985, geologists warned that a Columbian volcano, Nevado del Ruiz, was getting ready to erupt. But government officials and inhabitants of nearby towns did not take the warnings seriously. After all, the volcano had been dormant for 150 years. On the evening of November 13, Nevado del Ruiz erupted, triggering catastrophic mudslides. In the town of Armero, 23,000 people were buried alive in a matter of seconds.

For ninety percent of the last million years, the normal state of the Earth's climate has been an Ice Age. Ice ages last about 100,000 years, and are punctuated by short periods of warm climate, or interglacials. The last Ice Age started about 114,000 years ago. It began instantaneously. For a hundred-thousand years, temperatures fell and sheets of ice a mile thick grew to envelop much of North America, Europe and Asia. The Ice Age ended nearly as abruptly as it began. Between about 12,000 and 10,000 years ago, temperature in Greenland rose more than 50 °F.

We don't know what causes Ice Ages to begin or end. In 1875, a janitor turned geologist, James Croll, proposed that small variations in Earth's orbit around the Sun were responsible for climate change. This idea enjoyed its greatest heyday during the 1970s, when ocean sediment cores appeared to confirm the theory. But in 1992, Ike Winograd and his colleagues at the U.S. Geological Survey falsified the theory by demonstrating that its predictions were inconsistent with new, high-quality data.

The climate of the Ice Age is documented in the ice layers of Greenland and Antarctica. We have cored these layers, extracted them, and studied them in the laboratory. Not only were Ice Ages significantly colder than today, but the climates were considerably more variable. Compared to the norm of the last million years, we live in a climate that is remarkably warm, stable and benign. During the last Ice Age in Greenland abrupt climatic swings of 30 °F were common. Since the Ice Age ended, variations of 3 °F are uncommon.

For thousands of years people have learned from experience that cold temperatures are detrimental for human welfare and warm temperatures are beneficial. From about 1300 to 1800 AD, the climate cooled slightly during a period known as the Little Ice Age. The advent of the Little Ice Age was marked by the Black Death, the largest disaster ever to hit the human race. One-third of humanity perished; terror and anarchy prevailed. In Greenland, the temperature fell by about 4 °F. Although trivial, compared to an Ice Age cooling of 50 °F, this was nevertheless sufficient to wipe out the Viking colony there. Human civilization as we know it is only possible in a warm interglacial climate. Short of a catastrophic asteroid impact, the greatest threat to humanity is the onset of the next Ice Age.

The oscillation between Ice Ages and interglacial periods is the dominant feature of Earth's climate for the last million years. But the meteorological computer models that predict significant global warming from carbon dioxide cannot reproduce these temperature changes. This failure to reproduce the most significant aspect of terrestrial climate reveals an incomplete understanding of the climate system, if not a nearly complete ignorance.

Global warming predictions by meteorologists are based on speculative, untested, and poorly constrained computer models. But our knowledge of Ice Ages is based on a wide variety of indisputable data, including cores from the Greenland and Antarctic ice sheets. In this instance, it would be perspicacious to listen to the geologists, not the meteorologists. It would be a terrible mistake to hasten the advent of the next Ice Age by reducing our production of carbon dioxide. Yet this is exactly what we are planning on doing.

The coldest part of the Little Ice Age during the latter half of the seventeenth century, was marked by the nearly complete absence of sunspots. The Sun is the engine that drives our climate. Every other factor is trivial. And the Sun appears to be entering a new period of quiescence. August 2008 was the first month since the year 1913 that no sunspots were observed. As I write, the sun remains quiet. Over the last two years, mean global temperatures have fallen significantly. The Earth is now no warmer than it was in 1995.

Nature has an inevitable way of asserting itself. It is only our hubris that makes us think we can master nature's mysteries or control the climate.

14 GLOBAL WARMING IS OVER

In 2008, President-elect Barack Obama declared his intention to mitigate global warming by enacting a cap-and-trade policy that would reduce carbon emissions eighty percent by the year 2050. But the last two years of global cooling have nearly erased thirty years of temperature increases. To the extent that global warming ever existed, it is now officially over.

2008 began with a severe spell of winter weather in China. Observers characterized it as the largest natural disaster to hit that country in decades. By the end of January, blizzards and cold temperatures had killed 60 people and caused millions to lose electric service. Nearly a million buildings were damaged and airports had to close. Hong Kong had the second-longest cold spell since 1885. A temperature of 33.6 °F was barely higher than the record low of 32.0 °F set in 1893.

Other countries in Asia also experienced record cold. In February, cold temperatures in the northern half of Vietnam wiped out 40 percent of the rice crop and killed 33,000 head of livestock. In India, the city of Mumbai recorded the lowest temperatures of the past forty years. Across India, there was more frost damage to crops than at any other time in the past thirty years.

In the United States, the weather was also frigid. The city of International Falls, Minnesota, whose official nickname is the "icebox of the nation," set a new record low temperature of -40 °F, breaking the old record of -37 °F established in 1967. Alaska experienced an unusually cold and wet summer. For the first time since the 18th century, Alaskan glaciers grew instead of retreating. In Fairbanks, the month of October was the fourth coldest in 104 years of record. Last month in Reading, Pennsylvania, the temperature stayed below 40 °F for six consecutive days--the longest November cold spell there since 1903.

These cold weather events were not anomalous or isolated incidents. Global measures of climatic conditions indicate significant cooling. According to a preliminary estimate by the British Met Office, 2008 will be the coldest year of the last ten. The extent of global sea ice is at the same level it was in 1980. The mean planetary temperature, as monitored by satellite, is also the same as it was in the year 1980. Last March, NASA reported that the oceans have been cooling for the last five years. Sea level has stopped rising, and cyclone and hurricane activity in the northern hemisphere is at a 24-year low.

Environmental extremists and global warming alarmists are in denial and running for cover. Their rationale for continuing a lost cause is that weather events in the short term are not necessarily related to long term climatic trends. But these are the same people who screamed at us each year that ordinary weather events such as high temperatures or hurricanes were undeniable evidence of imminent doom.

Now that global warming is over, politicians are finally ready to enact dubious solutions to a non-existent problem. In Britain, Parliament is intrepidly forging ahead with a bold new plan to cool the climate, even as London experienced its first October snowfall since 1934, and Ireland went through the coldest October in the last 70 years. This is an absurd spectacle. Our advanced civilization is being systematically mismanaged by technologically illiterate lawyers responding to political pressures from irrational fanatics. Would someone please tell these people that it is impossible to overturn the laws of thermodynamics?

We cannot improve our economy by artificially forcing people to use expensive, unreliable, and inefficient energy sources. Let the politicians take note. People will not like what you have in mind. California is arguably the most liberal state in the nation. Yet last month they defeated, by nearly a two-to-one margin, a law that would have forced California utilities to obtain half their electric power from renewable sources. What the Obama administration is proposing is much more radical than this. Their cap-and-trade proposal will dramatically increase the energy costs of the average consumer and likely drive our crippled economy into a severe depression.

To the extent that global warming was ever valid, it is now officially over. It is time to file this theory in the dustbins of history, next to Aristotelean physics, Neptunism, the Geocentric Universe, phlogiston, and a plethora of other incorrect scientific theories, all of which had vocal and dogmatic supporters who cited incontrovertible evidence. Weather and climate change are natural processes beyond human control. To argue otherwise is to deny the factual evidence.

15 SCIENCE IS NEVER SETTLED

President Obama has said that the science of global warming is settled. Former vice-president Al Gore has gone so far as to state that doubting the alleged consensus on global warming is equivalent to maintaining that the Earth is flat. But these statements by Obama and Gore only illustrate that they don't understand science. "Settled science" is an oxymoron, and anyone who characterizes science as "settled" is ignorant not only of science, but also history and philosophy.

Aristotle, who lived and wrote in the 4th century BC, was one of the greatest geniuses the world has ever known. He invented the discipline of logic and founded the sciences of ecology and biology. Aristotle's physics was accepted as correct for nearly two thousand years. In 1534, faculty at the University of Paris officially asserted that the works of Aristotle were "the standard and basis of all philosophic enquiry."

Aristotle taught that heavy objects fall faster than light ones. Over the centuries, a few unreasonable persons expressed skeptical concerns. But the consensus was that the physics of motion were described by Aristotle's dicta. The science was settled.

Around the year 1591, an irascible young instructor at the University of Pisa demonstrated that Aristotle was wrong. He climbed to the top of the tower of Pisa and dropped cannon balls of unequal weight that hit the ground simultaneously. Aristotelean professors on the faculty were embarrassed. The University administration responded by not renewing Galileo's contract, thus ridding themselves of a troublemaker who challenged the accepted consensus.

Galileo is better remembered today for clashing with the Catholic Church over the issue of whether or not the Earth was at the center of the universe. An Earth-centered cosmology was first proposed by the Greek philosopher,

Eudoxus, in the 4th century BC. About a hundred years later, an upstart named Aristarchus suggested that the Earth revolved around the Sun. Aristarchus' system never proved popular, and he was criticized for being impious.

The Earth-centered system was finalized by Claudius Ptolemy in the second century AD, and remained unchallenged until the sixteenth century. Everyone knew that the science of astronomy had been "settled." When Galileo insisted that the Earth revolved around the Sun he was castigated by the Church for advocating an idea that was not only heretical, but also "foolish and absurd in philosophy."

Late in the seventeenth century, Isaac Newton demonstrated definitively that Aristotle's physics was incorrect. He proposed the Law of Universal Gravitation, and explained how the planets move around the Sun in elliptical orbits. Newton is still regarded as the greatest scientist who ever lived. He settled the science of motion in such a conclusive way that his system was referred to as an "invincible edifice." But the edifice crumbled early in the twentieth century when Einstein showed that Newtonian physics breaks down as the speed of light is approached.

Even Newton made mistakes in physics. In a letter addressed to Robert Hooke, Newton noted that if a body could fall to the center of the Earth it would follow a spiral path. But Hooke knew that the path would be elliptical, because he had conducted experiments with pendulums and rolled balls inside various surfaces of revolution. Confronted with Hooke's rebuttal, Newton was forced to acknowledge his error.

Near the beginning of the nineteenth century, the Neptunian School of geology taught that all rocks had formed by crystallization from a now-vanished universal ocean. Although the evidence falsifying this theory was both plain and abundant, Neptunists interpreted every observation as supportive of their hypothesis. Blinded by an immoderate zeal, they selected and magnified any fact in accordance with their theory, while neglecting those that tended to disprove it. Robert Jameson characterized the evidence supporting Neptunism as "incontrovertible." But the theory collapsed in a few decades, and today is recognized as an artifact of inexhaustible human folly.

Mr. Gore and Mr. Obama would now have us believe that the process of history has stopped. For the first time, scientific knowledge is not provisional and subject to revision, but final and settled. Skepticism, which has been the spur to all innovation and human progress, is unacceptable and must be condemned.

But in fact, it is our awareness of what we do not know that determines our scientific level. Socrates was the wisest man, not because he knew more than others, but because he was the only one to recognize that he did not know. Knowledge begins with skepticism and ends with conceit.

16 GLOBAL WARMING IS A FRAUD

As the years pass and data accumulate, it is becoming evident that global warming is a fraud. Climate change is natural and ongoing, but the Earth has not warmed significantly over the last thirty years. Nor has there been a single negative effect of any type that can be unambiguously attributed to global warming.

As I write, satellite data show that the mean global temperature is the same that it was in 1979. The extent of global sea ice is also unchanged from 1979. Since the end of the last Ice Age, sea level has risen more than a hundred meters. But for the last three years, there has been no rise in sea level. If the polar ice sheets are melting, why isn't sea level rising? Global warming is supposed to increase the severity and frequency of tropical storms. But hurricane and typhoon activity is at a record low.

Every year in the US, more than forty thousand people are killed in traffic accidents. But not one single person has ever been killed by global warming. The number of species that have gone extinct from global warming is exactly zero. Both the Antarctic and Greenland Ice Sheets are stable. The polar bear population is increasing. There has been no increase in infectious disease that can be attributed to climate change. We are not currently experiencing more floods, droughts, or forest fires.

In short, there is no evidence of any type to support the idea that we are entering an era when significant climate change is occurring and will cause the deterioration of either the natural environment or the human standard of living.

Why do people think the planet is warming? One reason is that the temperature data from weather stations appear to be hopelessly contaminated by urban heat effects. A survey of the 1221 temperature stations in the US by meteorologist Anthony Watts and his colleagues is now more than 80 percent complete. The magnitude of putative global warming over the last 150 years is about 0.7 °C. But only 9 percent of meteorological stations in the US are likely to have temperature errors lower than 1 °C. More than two-thirds of temperature sensors used to estimate global warming are located near artificial heating sources such as air conditioning vents, asphalt paving, or buildings. These sources are likely to introduce artifacts greater than 2 °C into the temperature record.

Another cause of global warming hysteria is the infiltration of science by ideological zealots who place politics above truth. Earlier this month, the Obama administration issued a report that concluded global warming would have a number of deleterious effects on the US. In 1995, one of the lead authors of this report told me that we had to alter the historical temperature record by "getting rid" of the Medieval Warm Period.

The Obama report refers six times to the work of a climate scientist named Stephen H. Schneider. In 1989, Schneider told *Discover* magazine that "we have to offer up scary scenarios, make simplified, dramatic statements, and make little mention of any doubts we might have." Schneider concluded "each of us has to decide what the right balance is between being effective and being honest." Schneider's position is not unusual. In 2007, Mike Hulme, the founding director of the Tyndall Center for Climate Change Research in Britain, told the *Guardian* newspaper that "scientists and politicians must trade truth for influence."

While releasing a politicized report that prostitutes science to politics, the Obama administration simultaneously suppressed an internal EPA report that concluded there were "glaring inconsistencies" between the scientific data and the hypothesis that carbon dioxide emissions were changing the climate.

If we had an appreciation for history, we would not be fooled so easily. It has all happened before, albeit on a smaller scale in an age where people had more common sense. On May 19, 1912, the *Washington Post* posed these questions: "Is the climate of the world changing? Is it becoming warmer in the polar regions?" On November 2, 1922, the *Associated Press* reported that "the Arctic Ocean is warming up, icebergs are growing scarcer and in some places the seals are finding the waters too hot." On February 25, 1923, the *New York Times* concluded that "the Arctic appears to be warming up." On December 21, 1930, the *Times* noted that "Alpine glaciers are in full retreat." A few months later the *New York Times* concluded that there was "a radical change in climatic conditions and hitherto unheard of warmth" in Greenland. About the only thing that has changed at the *Times* since 1930 is that no one working there today is literate enough to use the word "hitherto."

After the warm weather of the 1930s gave way to a cooling trend beginning in 1940, the media began speculating on the imminent arrival of a new Ice Age. We have now come full circle, mired in a hopeless cycle of reincarnated ignorance. H. L. Mencken understood this process when he explained "the whole aim of practical politics is to keep the populace alarmed by an endless series of hobgoblins, most of them imaginary."

17 DEATH OF A CIVILIZATION

Over the past several years we have learned that small groups of people can engage in mass suicide. In 1978, 918 members of the Peoples' Temple led by Jim Jones perished after drinking poisoned Kool-Aid. In 1997, 39 members of the Heaven's Gate cult died after drugging themselves and tying plastic bags around their heads. Unfortunately, history also demonstrates that it is possible for an entire civilization to commit suicide by intentionally destroying the means of its subsistence.

In the early nineteenth century, the British colonized Southeast Africa. The native Xhosa resisted, but suffered repeated and humiliating defeats at the hands of British military forces. The Xhosa lost their independence and their native land became an English colony. The British adopted a policy of westernizing the Xhosa. They were to be converted to Christianity, and their native culture and religion was to be wiped out. Under the stress of being confronted by a superior and irresistible technology, the Xhosa developed feelings of inadequacy and inferiority. In this climate, a prophet appeared.

In April of 1856, a fifteen-year-old girl named Nongqawuse heard a voice telling her that the Xhosa must kill all their cattle, stop cultivating their fields, and destroy their stores of grain and food. The voice insisted that the Xhosa must also get rid of their hoes, cooking pots, and every utensil necessary for the maintenance of life. Once these things were accomplished, a new day would magically dawn. Everything necessary for life would spring spontaneously from the earth. The dead would be resurrected. The blind would see and the old would have their youth restored. New food and livestock would appear in abundance, spontaneously sprouting from the earth. The British would be swept into the sea, and the Xhosa would be restored to their former glory. What was promised was nothing less than the establishment of paradise on earth.

Nongqawuse told this story to her guardian and uncle, Mhlakaza. At first, the uncle was skeptical. But he became a believer after accompanying his niece to the spot where she heard the voices. Although Mhlakaza heard nothing, he became convinced that Nongqawuse was hearing the voice of her dead father, and that the instructions must be obeyed. Mhlakaza became the chief prophet and leader of the cattle-killing movement.

News of the prophecy spread rapidly, and within a few weeks the Xhosa king, Sarhili, became a convert. He ordered the Xhosa to slaughter their cattle and, in a symbolic act, killed his favorite ox. As the hysteria widened, other Xhosa began to have visions. Some saw shadows of the resurrected dead arising from the sea, standing in rushes on the river bank, or even floating in the air. Everywhere that people looked, they found evidence to support what they desperately wanted to be true.

The believers began their work in earnest. Vast amounts of grain were taken out of storage and scattered on the ground to rot. Cattle were killed so quickly and on such an immense scale that vultures could not entirely devour the rotting flesh. The ultimate number of cattle that the Xhosa slaughtered was 400,000. After killing their livestock, the Xhosa built new, larger kraals to hold the marvelous new beasts that they anticipated would rise out of the earth. The impetus of the movement became irresistible.

The resurrection of the dead was predicted to occur on the full moon of June, 1856. Nothing happened. The chief prophet of the cattle-killing movement, Mhlakaza, moved the date to the full moon of August. But again the prophecy was not fulfilled.

The cattle-killing movement now began to enter a final, deadly phase, which its own internal logic dictated as inevitable. The failure of the prophecies was blamed on the fact that the cattle-killing had not been completed. Most believers had retained a few cattle, chiefly consisting of milk cows that provided an immediate and continuous food supply. Worse yet, there was a minority community of skeptical non-believers who refused to kill their livestock.

The fall planting season came and went. Believers threw their spades into the rivers and did not sow a single seed in the ground. By December of 1856, the Xhosa began to feel the pangs of hunger. They scoured the fields and woods for berries and roots, and attempted to eat bark stripped from trees. Mhlakaza set a new date of December 11 for the fulfillment of the prophecy. When the anticipated event did not occur, unbelievers were blamed.

The resurrection was rescheduled yet again for February 16, 1857, but the believers were again disappointed. Even this late, the average believer still had three or four head of livestock alive. The repeated failure of the prophecies could only mean that the Xhosa had failed to fulfill the necessary requirement of killing every last head of cattle. Now, they finally began to complete the killing process. Not only cattle were slaughtered, but also chickens and goats. Any viable means of sustenance had to be destroyed. Any cattle that might have escaped earlier killing were now slaughtered for food.

Serious famine began in late spring of 1857. All the food was gone. The starving population broke into stables and ate horse food. They gathered bones that had lay bleaching in the sun for years and tried to make soup. They ate grass. Maddened by hunger, some resorted to cannibalism. Weakened by starvation, family members often had to lay and watch dogs devour the corpses of their spouses and children. Those who did not die directly from hunger fell prey to disease. To the end, true believers never renounced their faith. They simply starved to death, blaming the failure of the prophecy on the doubts of non-believers.

By the end of 1858, the Xhosa population had dropped from 105,000 to 26,000. Forty to fifty-thousand people starved to death, and the rest migrated. With Xhosa civilization destroyed, the land was cleared for white settlement. The British found that those Xhosa who survived proved to be docile and useful servants. What the British Empire had been unable to accomplish in more than fifty years of aggressive colonialism, the Xhosa did to themselves in less than two years.

Western civilization now stands on the brink of repeating the experience of the Xhosa. Since the advent of the Industrial Revolution in the late eighteenth century, Europe and North America have enjoyed the greatest prosperity ever known on earth. Life expectancy has doubled. In a little more than two hundred years, every objective measure of human welfare has increased more than in all of previous human history.

But Western Civilization is coasting on an impetus provided by our ancestors. There is scarcely anyone alive in Europe or America today who believes in the superiority of Western society. Guilt and shame hang around our necks like millstones, dragging our emasculated culture to the verge of self-immolation. Whatever faults the British Empire-builders may have had, they were certain of themselves.

Our forefathers built a technological civilization based on energy provided by carbon-based fossil fuels. Without the inexpensive and reliable energy provided by coal, oil, and gas, our civilization would quickly collapse. The prophets of global warming now want us to do precisely that.

Like the prophet Mhlakaza, Al Gore promises that if we stop using carbon-based energy, new energy technologies will magically appear. The laws of physics and chemistry will be repealed by political will power. We will achieve prosperity by destroying the very means by which prosperity is created.

While Western Civilization sits confused, crippled with self-doubt and guilt, the Chinese are rapidly building an energy-intensive technological civilization. They have 2,000 coal-fired power plants, and are currently constructing new ones at the rate of one a week. In China, more people believe in free-market economics than in the US. Our Asian friends are about to be nominated by history as the new torchbearers of human progress.

18 GLOBAL WARMING AND THE AGE OF THE EARTH: A LESSON ON THE NATURE OF SCIENTIFIC KNOWLEDGE

The world stands on the verge of committing itself to limits on the emission of carbon dioxide that would drastically reduce the use of fossil fuels. If this fateful decision is made, the economies of developed nations will be strangled. Human prosperity will be reduced. Our ability to solve pressing problems, both human and environmental, will be severely limited. We have been told that these shackles must be imposed to forestall a hypothetical global warming projected to occur some time in the distant future. But to date the only unambiguous evidence for planetary warming is a modest rise in temperature (less than one degree Celsius) that falls well within the range of natural variation.

The validity of warming predictions depends upon the questionable reliability of computer models of the climate system. But Earth's climate system is complex and poorly understood. And the integrity of the computer models cannot be demonstrated or even tested. To anyone with an awareness of the nature and limitations of scientific knowledge, it must appear that the human race is repeating a foolish mistake from the past. We have been down this road before, most notably in the latter half of the nineteenth century when it appeared that mathematics and physics had conclusively answered the question of the Earth's age. At that time, a science that had been definitely "settled" fell apart in the space of a few years. The mathematical models that appeared to be so certain proved to be completely, even ridiculously wrong.

The age of the Earth is one of the great questions that has puzzled people for thousands of years. In *Meteorologica*, Aristotle (384-322 BC) asserted that the world was eternal. But with the advent of Christianity and Islam, scholars began to assume that humanity was coeval with the Creation of the world. It followed that the age of the Earth could be estimated from a careful examination of sacred writings.

The first person to make a quantitative estimate of the Earth's age was the Islamic scientist al-Biruni (c. 973-1050). al-Biruni based his chronology on the Hindu, Jewish, and Christian religious scriptures. He divided the history of the world into eras, and concluded that it had been less than ten thousand years since the Creation.

Working in the tradition begun by al-Biruni, Bishop James Ussher (1581-1686) estimated the age of the Earth by meticulously studying the Bible and other historical documents. In *The Annals of the World Deduced from the Origin of Time*, Ussher pinpointed the date of Creation as the "night preceding the 23rd of October, 4004 BC." Ussher's scholarship was impressive, and his dates were accepted as the standard chronology. Bible editors began to place Ussher's dates in the margins of their texts.

Isaac Newton (1642-1727), the greatest scientist of the age, was also a Biblical fundamentalist who believed in a young Earth. Newton explained to his nephew, John Conduitt, that the Earth could not be old because all human technology was of recent invention. Like Ussher, Newton wrote his own universal history, *Chronology of Ancient Kingdoms Amended*, that was published posthumously in 1728.

The procedures for establishing a scientific estimate of the age of the Earth were laid out in the seventeenth century by the Danish anatomist, Nicolaus Steno (1638-1686). Steno was the first person to state unequivocally that the history of the Earth was not to be found in human chronicles, but in the Earth itself. Steno's principles of geologic investigation became the basis for establishing the relative age of rock sequences and the foundation of historical geology.

Armed with Steno's principles, eighteenth century naturalists began to seriously consider the implications of the rock record. It became apparent to them that an immense amount of time was required to deposit the rock layers that covered the Earth's surface.

One of the first to recognize the scope of geologic time was the Scottish philosopher James Hutton (1726-1797). In the year 1788, Hutton was accompanied on a field trip by his friend, the mathematician, John Playfair (1748-1819). They traveled up the coastline of Scotland to Siccar Point, and Hutton described the history implied by the sequence of rocks exposed there. After listening to Hutton's exposition, Playfair later wrote "the mind seemed to grow giddy by looking so far into the abyss of time."

By the time Charles Darwin (1809-1882) published *Origin of Species* in 1859, geologists were of the opinion that the Earth was practically, although not literally, of infinite age. With infinite time at this disposal, Darwin was able to invoke the slow mechanism of natural selection as an explanation for the organic evolution evidenced in the fossil record.

To demonstrate the vast extent of geologic time, Darwin offered the erosion of the Weald, a seaside cliff in England, as an offhand example. Darwin assumed an erosion rate of an inch a century, and then extrapolated that some 300 million years were apparently necessary to explain the total amount of erosion that had occurred.

But Darwin's estimated erosion rate of one inch per century was little more than speculation. The number was unconstrained by any measurement or scientific observation. Nineteenth-century geologists lacked any quantitative method for establishing dates. The rocks of the Earth's crust might represent the passage of ten million years. But just as easily, the amount of time could have been a hundred, a thousand, or ten thousand million years.

Darwin and his geological colleagues were soon taken to the woodshed by the greatest physicist of the nineteenth century, William Thomson (1824-1907). Better known as Lord Kelvin, Thomson was a man of prodigious gifts who possessed enormous intellectual stature. He published his first scientific paper at age sixteen, and had been appointed a chaired professor at the University of Glasgow at the precocious age of twenty-two.

In 1861, Lord Kelvin began to seriously address the question of dating the Earth. He was aware that the Earth radiated internal heat. This process could not have been going on forever. By maintaining that the Earth was infinitely old, the geologists in effect were postulating that energy was not conserved. This violated the First Law of Thermodynamics, and Kelvin was aroused to do battle.

In the nineteenth century, the only known source for the internal heat of the Earth was the original mechanical heat of accretion. Reasoning that the Earth had been molten at the time of its formation, but cooling ever since, Kelvin was able to construct an elegant mathematical model that constrained the age of the Earth on the basis of its measured geothermal gradient. Much the same method is used today by coroners who estimate the time of death by taking the temperature of a cadaver.

In 1862, Kelvin published his analysis in a paper titled *On the Secular Cooling of the Earth*. He arrived at a best estimate for the age of the Earth of 100 million years. Kelvin's estimate was no idle speculation. It was based on a precise mathematical model constrained by laboratory measurements and the laws of thermodynamics.

Kelvin attacked Darwin directly. He raised the question: were the laboratory measurements and mathematical calculations in error, or was it more likely "that a stormy sea, with possibly channel tides of extreme violence, should encroach on a chalk cliff 1,000 times more rapidly than Mr. Darwin's estimate of one inch per century?"

Darwin was devastated. He wrote to his mentor, Charles Lyell, "for heaven's sake take care of your fingers; to burn them severely, as I have done, is very unpleasant." Geologists were left sputtering. They had no effective rebuttal to Kelvin's calculations. Within a few years, the geological establishment began to line up with Lord Kelvin. Among the influential converts was Archibald Geikie, President of both the British Association for the Advancement of Science and the Geological Society of London.

Researchers began to look for evidence that would confirm Kelvin's calculations. In 1865, Geologist Samuel Haughton had estimated the age of the Earth as 2300 million years, a number reasonably close to the modern value of 4500 million years. But under the influence of Kelvin's authority, in 1878 Haughton drastically shortened his earlier calculation to 153 million years.

A lone voice of dissent was raised by the biologist, Thomas Huxley (1825-1895). Huxley pointed out that there was a fundamental weakness in Kelvin's mathematical model. "Mathematics may be compared to a mill of exquisite workmanship, which grinds you stuff of any degree of fineness; but, nevertheless, what you get out depends on what you put in." Put in more modern terms, Huxley's observation amounted to "garbage in, garbage out."

But as the end of the nineteenth century approached, the scientific community was beginning to regard Kelvin's estimate of 100 million years as a near certainty. Writing in the *American Journal of Science* in 1893, geologist Warren Upham characterized Kelvin's estimate of the age of the Earth as the most "important conclusion in the natural sciences...[that] has been reached during this century."

The science was definitely settled in 1899 by the Irish physicist, John Joly (1857-1933). Joly hit upon a robust method for calculating the age of the Earth that was entirely different from Kelvin's. Joly's calculation was childishly simple, yet apparently foolproof. He estimated the age of the Earth by dividing the total salt content of the oceans by the rate at which salt was being carried to the sea by the rivers. He found that it would take 80 to 90 million years for the ocean's salt to accumulate.

In consideration of the uncertainties involved, Joly's age estimate was essentially identical to Thomson's. With different methods yielding the same result, it seemed evident that the result was conclusive: the Earth was 100 million years old. It seemed that to deny this reality, was to deny not only the authority of the scientific establishment but the very laws of nature themselves.

The ingenious calculations of Kelvin and Joly were soon to be overturned by an improbable empiricism. In the thirteenth century, modern science began when philosophers came to the realization that logic alone could never uncover the secrets of the cosmos, no matter how seductive its appeal. Contemplation of the mysterious properties of the magnet convinced Roger Bacon and his contemporaries that nature contained occult or hidden forces that could never be discerned or anticipated rationally, only discovered experimentally.

In 1896, Henri Becquerel accidentally discovered radioactivity when he found that photographic plates were exposed when placed next to certain minerals. By 1904, it became apparent that there were radioactive minerals inside the Earth releasing heat. Lord Kelvin's assumption of no internal heat sources was wrong. At the beginning of the twentieth century, it was not even clear if the Earth was cooling or heating. Thomson's calculations were precise, but he had no way of knowing about radioactivity.

Radioactivity also provided a rigorous way to calculate the age of the Earth. The accepted modern estimate for the age of the Earth is 4500 million years. The nineteenth-century estimate of 100 million years that seemed so certain was wrong, not just by 20 or 30 percent, but by a factor of 45. In retrospect, the reason that Thomson's estimates had been independently confirmed is that geologists looked for data that would support Thomson's physics. The consensus that had emerged was the product of a human psychological process, not objective science. The nature of science is such that people who look for confirming evidence will always find it.

Compared to modern climate models, William Thomson's models were simple, and contained only a few assumptions. In contrast, global warming models are hideously complex, and contain numerous hidden assumptions, many of which are highly uncertain. The most significant of these is whether water vapor will exert a negative or positive feedback on the warming induced by carbon dioxide. All the major climate models assume the feedback will be positive, exaggerating any possible warming. But recent research indicates the feedback may be negative. We don't know.

There is also much we do not understand about why Earth's climate changes. It is possible that cosmic rays, modulated by the Sun's magnetic field, cool Earth by inducing the formation of clouds. We don't know why Ice Ages end so spectacularly and suddenly. Once they begin, Ice Ages should continue indefinitely, as cooling is reinforced by a number of positive feedbacks.

We ought to be intelligent enough to acknowledge that we don't know what we don't know. Science is *never* settled. We should keep in mind Seneca's admonition. "Nature does not reveal all her secrets at once. We imagine we are initiated in her mysteries: we are, as yet, but hanging around her outer courts."

There has never been a time when the need for understanding the limits and nature of scientific knowledge is so compelling, or the ramifications of ignorance so consequential. Those who ignore history are apt to repeat its mistakes.

19 THE PROBLEMS WITH AL GORE

Al Gore has publicly stated that people who are skeptical of the hysterical global warming scenario he has been promoting (and profiting from) are comparable to the lunatic fringe who believe that the Apollo Moon landings were filmed on a backstage lot in Arizona. He has also compared global warming skeptics to people who believe the Earth is flat.

The implication is that global warming skeptics like myself are not just misinformed, but are cranks with psychological problems. Skeptics have also been called "deniers," as if we were unreasonably denying an uncontroverted fact. In 2007, Boston Globe columnist Ellen Goodman stated "the poles are melting" (they weren't and aren't) and scathingly concluded that "global warming deniers are now on a par with Holocaust deniers."

On December 6, 2006, I testified before the US Senate that media bias over global warming had "bloomed into irrational hysteria." When I returned to Oklahoma, I discovered a new way to spell the word "professor." On an internet news group, someone who had heard my testimony posted "scoundrelous little Dust Bowl professorwhore David Deming is the latest in a long line of professwhores bribed by Big Oil to lie massively in front of TV cameras."

But I've never received money from any energy company. No money from coal, no money from petroleum, and no money from the natural gas industry. Petroleum companies donate lots of money to the environmental groups that hate them, but give little to nothing to deniers like me. Like other "deniers," my reward for honest science has so far amounted to generous donations of lies, calumnies, and personal attacks. In contrast, the scientists who promote global warming alarmism receive billions in research grants to produce bogus junk science. Honesty doesn't pay.

Al Gore has declared that the science of global warming is definitely settled, but puzzlingly refuses to engage in debates. Notably, Gore has repeatedly dodged a debate with Christopher Monckton. The question is self-evident. If the evidence for global warming is so overwhelming, why won't Gore use this opportunity to destroy his critics and advance his agenda? The answer is that Gore refuses to submit to any sort of critical examination because an open debate would reveal that he doesn't have a clue as to what he is talking about.

Al Gore recently proved himself to be an idiot by making some remarkably ignorant statements in a television interview. Promoting geothermal energy, Gore said that temperature in the interior of the Earth is "several *million* degrees." Oh, my, God. Since people first started lowering thermometers into boreholes in the nineteenth century, we have known that the temperature of the Earth's core is no more than several *thousand* degrees Celsius. The temperature at the inner-outer core boundary is constrained by a phase transition to be in the neighborhood of 6000 °C. More to the point, the temperature of near-surface rocks in geothermal areas is typically hundreds of °C. At temperatures exceeding 1000 °C in the Earth's crust, rock begins to melt. So Gore was wrong by at least a factor of a thousand, or by one-hundred-thousand percent.

Gore's blithe and erroneous characterization of the Earth's internal temperature was not an insignificant slip of the tongue. This man, a politician and lawyer, is now advising the world on energy and science policies. These are weighty areas that involve complex technical matters. But Gore's remarks reveal his ignorance of physics, chemistry, geology, and thermodynamics. The point is that widespread development of geothermal energy is not feasible precisely *because* Earth's internal temperatures are not as high as Gore believes. If you think that Gore's error was inconsequential, try introducing an error of one-hundred-thousand percent into the design of a nuclear power plant and see what happens.

But Al Gore is less than an idiot. He is a clueless idiot, because he followed up his imbecilic statement about temperature with an even more asinine remark. After declaring that temperatures inside the Earth are "several million degrees," Gore claimed that we have "new drill bits that don't melt in that heat." How can anyone be so stupid as to think we have metallurgical techniques capable of producing drill bits that don't melt in temperatures of "several million degrees?"

After getting the facts wrong, Gore made the stunning assertion that geothermal resources in the US alone are so enormous that they could meet our entire energy needs for 35,000 years. What a visionary! Is it not remarkable that we ignore such a vast, unexploited source of energy? Is it not astonishing that generations of scientists and engineers have failed to recognize the potential for withdrawing virtually limitless amounts of energy from the Earth?

If the promise of geothermal energy sounds too good to be true, the reason is that it's not true. Extracting geothermal energy is inherently an inefficient process because you have to work against the Second Law of Thermodynamics. It's easy to turn mechanical energy into heat, but difficult to efficiently reverse the process. Practical geothermal energy production is limited to exceptional areas like Iceland because the high temperatures necessary are found only in a very few locations.

Al Gore may be a clueless idiot, but he's not alone. The world is full of ignorant and stupid people. As a college professor, I interact constantly with students, many of whom are very concerned with global warming. But in my interactions I have invariably found that the more science a student knows, the more skeptical they are of the standard global warming alarmist scenario. Students majoring in engineering or physics have some appreciation for the scientific method and the uncertainties involved in understanding and predicting climate change. Unlike Gore, they also understand that the ability to develop alternative energy sources is limited by the laws of physics and chemistry, not political willpower.

Students who buy into global warming alarmism are almost always from non-technical majors such as journalism. They can't think quantitatively, critically, or analytically. They have no interest in, or appreciation for, facts. Accordingly, they are almost completely ignorant of any relevant facts. Their minds are immature and their thought processes undisciplined. They don't understand the difference between fact and opinion. One student recently told me that we have to stop using oil because global warming was caused by the heat given off by the combustion of fossil fuels.

A human being has to acquire some education and knowledge before they can begin to develop an appreciation for the extent of their own ignorance. But these global warming alarmists know nothing, and therefore believe they understand everything. Al Gore and his mindless horde of followers are cretinous luddites revolting against an advanced civilization which possesses technologies they can't understand and therefore resent.

If I have been too hard on Mr. Gore, I ought to close by noting that stupidity is the normal human condition, intelligence the exception. Al Gore is not the only clueless idiot. US President Barack Obama takes advice from Gore. And a group of Norwegian politicians recently distinguished themselves by awarding Nobel Prizes to both Gore and Obama. As Nobel Prize recipients, Gore and Obama have joined an elite group that includes Portuguese physician Egas Moniz. In 1949, Moniz was awarded the Nobel prize for medicine for devising an innovative procedure known as the frontal lobotomy. It seems fitting that Gore and Obama are grouped with Moniz, since their goal is to lobotomize human civilization.

20 GLOBAL WARMING HOAX COLLAPSES

I told you so. When I testified before the US Senate on Dec. 6, 2006, I stated that the public was "vastly misinformed" on global warming, and that "there is no sound scientific basis for predicting future climate change with any degree of certainty." Looks like I was right. Since the Climategate scandal broke, the global warming hoax has collapsed like a house of rotten cards.

The Earth has not warmed appreciably for the last decade. There is no significant evidence that our climate has changed, or that the mild warming of the last 150 years can be attributed to anything other than natural variation. The Poles aren't melting, polar bears are thriving, and last year's Atlantic hurricane season was below average in activity. And the bitter winter of 2009-2010 brought home to Oklahomans the undeniable truth that cold weather is inherently more inclement than warm. The Christmas eve blizzard of 2009 was directly responsible for the deaths of at least nine people, and seven more died as a result of the storm that peaked on January 29.

I received little thanks for telling the truth as I saw it. I was called a "professwhore," and a "denier" who didn't care about the environment or the future. I was accosted by angry students. The Provost at the University of Oklahoma removed my freshman geology course from the list of approved general education courses. And contrary to popular belief, I have received no money from any energy company.

In October of 2006, a group of senior meteorologists at OU publicly claimed that I was attempting to deliberately misinform people. But the Climategate emails demonstrate that it's not skeptics like myself who have been misleading and misinforming the public. Climate researchers conspired to suppress the publication of dissenting views. Data were distorted and hidden for political purposes. The IPCC, that supposed bastion of objective and reliable science, has been revealed to be a political body that tendentiously manipulates data for ideological reasons. And we are just now learning that some of the IPCC's wild predictions were not based upon scientific study, but upon speculative and self-serving claims invented by environmental advocacy groups.

The Oklahoma Climatological Survey is charged with providing the Legislature and people of Oklahoma with accurate information and forecasts on climatic trends. In October of 2007, the Climatological Survey released a statement on climate change. Modestly described as "a definitive statement on global climate change," this report asserted "the climate will continue to warm through the 21st century." Contemplate that while you're cherishing memories of shoveling snow off your driveway or chipping ice from your windshield.

We're not supposed to confuse weather with climate. But the 2007 proclamation by the Climatological Survey explicitly predicted "warmer winters" and "fewer cold-air outbreaks and extremes." The authors of the Survey report were *wrong*. The second half of 2009 was "exceptionally cool," and last October was the coldest October in Oklahoma since record keeping began in the year 1895.

While the Oklahoma Climatological Survey was wrong, guess what? Last September, the *Farmer's Almanac* accurately predicted that we would have a "bitterly cold" winter season in 2009-2010 with lots of snowfall. And that's exactly what happened. A supermarket tabloid was significantly more accurate than the entire staff of scientists at the Climatological Survey.

As a result of the misinformation provided by the Climatological Survey, Oklahoma was ill-prepared for the severe winter weather we are currently experiencing. Ironically, Ken Crawford (then State Climatologist) was one of the people who publicly accused me of deliberately misinforming people.

Why was professor Deming, a geologist, able to get it right, while the professional climatologists got it wrong? The Climatological Survey report relied upon junk science produced by the IPCC. Political ideology was substituted for science. And intolerance produces bad science. If the meteorologists had listened to me, they might have learned something. Instead, they closed their minds and asserted their pedantic authority. The Climatological Survey is left with a shameful and embarrassing debacle. The people and State of Oklahoma would have been better served by constructive engagement and collaboration.

21 WHY I DENY GLOBAL WARMING

I'm a denier for several reasons. There is no substantive evidence that the planet has warmed significantly or that any significant warming will occur in the future. If any warming does occur, it likely will be concentrated at higher latitudes and therefore be beneficial. Climate research has largely degenerated into pathological science, and the coverage of global warming in the media is tendentious to the point of being fraudulent. Anyone who is an honest and competent scientist must be a denier.

Have you ever considered how difficult it is to take the temperature of the planet Earth? What temperature will you measure? The air? The surface of the Earth absorbs more than twice as much incident heat from the Sun than the air. But if you measure the temperature of the surface, what surface are you going to measure? The solid Earth or the oceans? There is twice as much water as land on Earth. If you decide to measure water temperature, at what depth will you take the measurements? How will the time scale on which the deep ocean mixes with the shallow affect your measurements? And how, pray tell, will you determine what the average water temperature was for the South Pacific Ocean a hundred years ago? How will you combine air, land, and sea temperature measurements? Even if you use only meteorological measurements of air temperature, how will you compensate for changes in latitude, elevation, and land use?

Determining a mean planetary temperature is not straightforward, but an extremely complicated problem. Even the best data are suspect. Anthony Watts and his colleagues have surveyed 82.5 percent of stations in the U.S. Historical Climatology Network. They have found--shockingly--that over 70 percent of these stations are likely to be contaminated by errors greater than 2 deg C [3.6 deg F]. Of the remaining stations, 21.5 percent have inherent errors greater than 1 deg C. The alleged degree of global warming over the past 150 years is less than 1 deg C. Yet even in a technologically advanced country like the US, the inherent error in over 90 percent of the surveyed meteorological stations is greater than the putative signal. And these errors are not random, but systematically reflect a warming bias related to urbanization. Watts has documented countless instances of air temperature sensors located next to air conditioning vents or in the middle of asphalt parking lots. A typical scenario is that a temperature sensor that was in the middle of a pasture a hundred years ago is now surrounded by a concrete jungle. Urbanization has been a unidirectional process. It is entirely plausible--even likely--that all of the temperature rise that has been inferred from the data is an artifact that reflects the growth of urban heat islands.

The "denier" is portrayed as a person who refuses to accept the plain evidence of his senses. But in fact it is the alarmist who doesn't know what they are talking about. The temperature of the Earth and how it has varied over the past 150 years is poorly constrained. The person who thinks otherwise does so largely because they have no comprehension of the science. Most of these people have never done science or thought about the inherent difficulties and uncertainties involved.

And what is "global warming" anyway? As long ago as the fifth century BC, Socrates pointed out that intelligible definitions are a necessary precursor to meaningful discussions. The definition of the term "global warming" shifts with the context of the discussion. If you deny global warming, then you have denied the existence of the greenhouse effect, a reproducible phenomenon that can be studied analytically in the laboratory. But if you oppose political action, then global warming metamorphoses into a nightmarish and speculative planetary catastrophe. Coastal cities sink beneath a rising sea, species suffer from wholesale extinctions, and green pastures are turned into deserts of choking hot sand.

In fact, so-called "deniers" are not "deniers" but skeptics. Skeptics do not deny the existence of the greenhouse effect. Holding all other factors constant, the mean planetary air temperature ought to rise as the atmosphere accumulates more anthropogenic CO_2. Christopher Monckton recently reviewed the pertinent science and concluded that a doubling of CO_2 should result in a temperature increase of about 1 deg C. If this temperature increase mirrors those in the geologic past, most of it will occur at high latitudes. These areas will become more habitable for man, plants, and other animals. Biodiversity will increase. Growing seasons will lengthen. Why is this a bad thing?

Any temperature increase over 1 deg C for a doubling of CO_2 must come from a positive feedback from water vapor. Water vapor is the dominant greenhouse gas in Earth's atmosphere, and warm air holds more water than cold air. The theory is that an increased concentration of water vapor in the atmosphere will lead to a positive feedback that amplifies the warming from CO_2 by as much as a factor of three to five. But this is nothing more that speculation. Water vapor also leads to cloud formation. Clouds have a cooling effect. At the current time, no one knows if the feedback from water vapor will be positive or negative.

Global warming predictions cannot be tested with mathematical models. It is *impossible* to validate computer models of complex natural systems. The only way to corroborate such models is to compare model predictions with what will happen in a hundred years. And one such result by itself won't be significant because of the possible compounding effects of other variables in the climate system. The experiment will have to repeated over several one-hundred year cycles. In other words, the theory of catastrophic global warming cannot be tested or empirically corroborated in a human time frame.

It is hardly conclusive to argue that models are correct because they have reproduced past temperatures. I'm sure they have. General circulation models have so many degrees of freedom that it is possible to endlessly tweak them until the desired result is obtained. Hindsight is always 20-20. This tells us exactly nothing about a model's ability to accurately predict what will happen in the future.

The entire field of climate science and its coverage in the media is tendentious to the point of being outright fraudulent. Why is it that every media report on CO_2--an invisible gas--is invariably accompanied by a photograph of a smokestack emitting condensed water vapor and particulate matter? Even the cover of Al Gore's movie, *An Inconvenient Truth*, shows a smokestack. Could it be that its difficult to get people worked up about an invisible, odorless gas that is an integral component of the photosynthetic cycle? A gas that is essential to most animal and plant life on Earth? A gas that is emitted by their own bodies through respiration? So you have to deliberately mislead people by showing pictures of smoke to them. Showing one thing when you're talking about another is fraud. If the case for global warming alarmism is so settled, so conclusive, so irrefutable...why is it necessary to repeatedly resort to fraud?

A few years ago it was widely reported that the increased concentration of carbon dioxide in the atmosphere would cause poison ivy to grow faster. But of course carbon dioxide causes almost all plants to grow faster. And nearly all of these plants have beneficial human uses. Carbon dioxide fertilizes hundreds or thousands of human food sources. More CO_2 means trees grow faster. So carbon dioxide promotes reforestation and biodiversity. Its good for the environment. But none of this was reported. Instead, the media only reported that global warming makes poison ivy grow faster. And this is but one example of hundreds or thousands of such misleading reports. If sea ice in the Arctic diminishes, it is cited as irrefutable proof of global warming. But if sea ice in the Antarctic increases, it is ignored. Even cold weather events are commonly invoked as evidence for global warming. People living in the future will look back and wonder how we could have been so delusional.

For the past few years I have remained silent concerning the Climategate emails. But what they revealed is what many of us already knew was going on: global warming research has largely degenerated into what is known as pathological science, a "process of wishful data interpretation." When I testified before the US Senate in 2006, I stated that a major climate researcher told me in 1995 that "we have to get rid of the Medieval Warm Period." The existence and global nature of the Medieval Warm Period had been substantiated by literally hundreds of research articles published over decades. But it had to be erased from history for ideological reasons. A few years later the infamous "hockey stick" appeared. The "hockey stick" was a revisionist attempt to rewrite the temperature history of the last thousand years. It has been discredited as being deeply flawed.

In one Climategate email, a supposed climate scientist admitted to "hiding the decline." In other words, hiding data that tended to disprove his ideological agenda. Another email described how alarmists would try to keep critical manuscripts from being published in the peer-reviewed scientific literature. One of them wrote, we'll "keep them out somehow -- even if we have to redefine what the peer-review literature is!" Gee. If the climate science that validates global warming is so unequivocal, why is it necessary to work behind the scenes to suppress dissent? You "doth protest too much."

As described in my book, *Science and Technology in World History: The Ancient World and Classical Civilization*, systematic science began with the invocation of naturalism by Greek philosophers and Hippocratic physicians c. 600-400 BC. But the critical attitude adopted by the Greeks was as important as naturalism. Students were not only allowed to criticize their teachers, but were encouraged to do so. From its beginnings in Greek natural philosophy, science has been an idealistic and dispassionate search for truth. As Plato explained, anyone who could point out a mistake "shall carry off the palm, not as an enemy, but as a friend." This is one reason that scientists enjoy so much respect. The public assumes that a scientist's pursuit of truth is unencumbered by political agendas.

But science does not come easy to men. "Science," George Sarton reminded us, "is a joykiller." The proper conduct of science requires a high degree of intellectual discipline and rigor. Scientists are supposed to use multiple working hypotheses and sort through these by the processes of corroboration and falsification. The most valuable evidence is that which tends to falsify or disprove a theory. A scientist, by the very definition of his activity, must be skeptical. A scientist engaged in a dispassionate search for truth elevates the critical--he does not suppress it. Knowledge begins with skepticism and ends with conceit.

Finally, I'm happy to be known as a "denier" because the label of "denier" says nothing about me, but everything about the person making the charge. Scientific theories are never denied or believed, they are only corroborated or falsified. Scientific knowledge, by its very nature, is provisional and subject to revision. The provisional nature of scientific knowledge is a necessary consequence of the epistemological basis of science. Science is based on observation. We never have all the data. As our body of data grows, our theories and ideas must necessarily evolve. Anyone who thinks scientific knowledge is final and complete must necessarily endorse as a corollary the absurd proposition that the process of history has stopped.

A scientific theory cannot be "denied." Only a belief can be denied. The person who uses the word "denier" thus reveals that they hold global warming as a belief, not a scientific theory. Beliefs are the basis of revealed religion. Revelations cannot be corroborated or studied in the laboratory, so religions are based on dogmatic beliefs conservatively held. Religions tend to be closed systems of belief that reject criticism. But the sciences are open systems of knowledge that welcome criticism. I'm a scientist, and therefore I must happily confess to being a denier.

22 MALTHUS RECONSIDERED

In *An Essay on the Principle of Population*, first published in 1798, Thomas Malthus stated his aphorism that the geometric growth of population must eventually exceed the arithmetic growth of resources. Malthus is most often considered or invoked in the context of acrimonious ideological debates on human population growth and its effect on the natural environment. In this brief paper I reconsider Malthus from a purely scientific viewpoint.

The gist of Malthus' argument was that the exponential growth of population must eventually outstrip the linear growth of resources.

> I say, that the power of population is indefinitely greater than the power in the earth to produce subsistence for man. Population, when unchecked, increases in a geometrical ratio. Subsistence increases only in an arithmetical ratio. A slight acquaintance with numbers will show the immensity of the first power in comparison of the second.

A corollary to Malthus' thesis is that humanity must perpetually exist in a state of misery, as population tends to invariably expand to the point that food supplies are at the subsistence level.

> And it [my hypothesis] appears, therefore, to be decisive against the possible existence of a society, all the members of which, should live in ease, happiness, and comparative leisure; and feel no anxiety about providing the means of subsistence for themselves and their families.

Malthus' contention that exponential growth must eventually outstrip arithmetic growth is frequently illustrated with trite examples such as guppies in a fish tank. It is often falsely assumed that exponential growth necessarily implies fast growth. In the 1972 book *Limits to Growth* the authors stated "exponential increase is deceptive because it generates immense numbers very quickly."

But this claim is *false*. Exponential growth is *not* necessarily faster than linear growth, nor is it true that exponential growth must eventually exceed linear. Both exponential and linear growth can be fast or slow. The doubling time for a population can be 25 years--or it can be 25,000 years; both growth rates are exponential. No matter how slow a growth rate you pick for an arithmetic function, I can find an exponential function with a slower growth rate whose total growth is less for any finite period of time. Arbitrary exponential growth only exceeds arithmetic growth for one uninteresting case: infinite time. Thus Malthus' thesis is not a tautology.

Malthus' thesis can also be tested as a scientific hypothesis. Malthus himself said "a just theory will always be confirmed by experiment." As it has been more than two hundred years since Malthus first published, it would seem that enough time has passed to determine whether or not Malthus was correct. From 1800 to 2000, world population increased from about 1 to 6 billion. According to Malthus' thesis, per capita food consumption for the world should now be lower than in 1800.

Historical food-production data are difficult to find, but proxies indicate that per capita food production has increased over the last two hundred years. From 1600 through 1974, the percentage of the population in Great Britain employed in agriculture dropped from 67% to about 6%. From 1800 through 1990, the price of wheat in the United States expressed in terms of wages decreased by a factor of 25. From 1800 to 2000, the population of England and Wales increased from about 9 million to more than 50 million while the inflation-adjusted price of wheat fell by more than a factor of ten. From 1961 through 1998, the world population increased from 3.1 billion to 5.9 billion. Over the same period of time the average daily per capita consumption of food calories in the world increased from 2250 to 2800. All of the preceding facts falsify Malthus' hypothesis.

Empirical falsifications of Malthus' proposition are often met by the criticism that not enough time has yet passed for population growth to outstrip food production. The question then presents itself: how much time is necessary to test the hypothesis? Is two hundred years not enough? A hallmark of scientific hypotheses is that they make specific, risky predictions that can be falsified. If Malthus' hypothesis cannot be falsified for any finite value of time, then its scientific status is questionable.

How could Malthus have been so wrong? Malthus did not foresee that the power of technology would enable resource growth to outstrip population growth. Malthus also did not anticipate the demographic transition that takes place when a society moves from an agricultural to a technological civilization. Malthus thought that when population growth was unrestrained (as it was in late 18th century North America) the population would double every 25 years. He noted that population increase in prosperous societies was a universal rule and called it an "incontrovertible truth." "That population does invariably increase, where there are the means of subsistence, the history of every people that have ever existed will abundantly prove."

In his memorable 1968 essay *Tragedy of the Commons*, Garrett Hardin noted that "there is no prosperous population in the world today that has, and has had for some time, a growth rate of zero." If that was true in 1968, it is no longer true today. As of 2010, Japan's rate of population growth is negative, and its total population is projected to decrease 26% by the year 2050. The population of Europe is also shrinking, and is projected to decrease from 740 to 725 million between 2010 and 2050.

As of 2010, the more developed regions of the world have a fertility rate of 1.7 births per woman, and a rate of natural population increase of only 0.2%. In the less developed areas of the world, the fertility rate has fallen dramatically and continues to decline. In the 1950s, the average woman in Africa, Asia, and Latin America gave birth to 6 children. But by 2010, the average fertility rate for the less developed areas of the world had fallen to 3.0 births per woman.

The decline in birth rates that accompanies a demographic transition is a happy circumstance that Malthus did not foresee. A number of reasons have been given for the lowering of birth rates that accompanies economic development. These include: (1) in agrarian societies, children are an economic asset, in technological societies they are an economic liability; (2) birth control has become increasingly available and culturally acceptable; (3) lower infant mortality; and (4) women in technological societies spend more time on education and work, and less time on childbearing and rearing.

In retrospect it is now apparent that one of the most important points in the history of human population growth took place in the interval 1962-1963. In those years the growth rate of the human population on Earth reached a maximum rate of 2.2% and started to decline. Since the early 1960s, the growth rate of world population has decreased in a uniform manner, reaching 1.2% in the year 2010. With the second derivative of the population growth curve turning and remaining negative, it seems probable that the world population will stabilize and perhaps even begin to decline before the end of this century.

Although Malthus and many others did not foresee the demographic transition in world population, it was predicted many decades ago by Edward

S. Deevey (1914-1988). In an analysis published in *Scientific American* in 1960, Deevey identified three surges in world population that had occurred throughout human time on Earth. The first expansion was initiated by the inventions of language, tool-making, and fire. The second population explosion started about 10,000 years ago when people began to abandon the hunter-gatherer lifestyle for agriculture and animal husbandry.

Deevey attributed the accelerating growth of the world population in 1960 to a decrease in the death rate caused by the scientific-industrial revolution. He noted that the growth of the human population in previous revolutions had followed an S-shaped curve, with a plateau inevitably following a period of rapid growth. With the perspective of all of human history to call on, Deevey calmly concluded that the current population explosion would be short-lived.

> Eventually the birth rate falls too, but not so fast, nor has it yet fallen so far as a bare replacement value. The natural outcome of this imbalance is that acceleration of annual increase which so bemuses demographers. In the long run it must prove to be temporary.

In the decades that followed, Deevey's calm and reasoned analysis was largely forgotten. Alarmed by the rapid growth of world population, neomalthusian prophets predicted catastrophic famines during the 1970s that never occurred.

The fact that Malthus was wrong should not be interpreted to suggest that a large human population is desirable, or that the root cause of environmental degradation is not the growth of the human population. We all understand that increases in human population are accompanied by environmental problems. I only suggest that it is time to put Malthus' morbid spectre of unrestrained population growth happily behind us and get on with the pleasant task of constructing the world that Malthus considered to be impossible.

23 ENVIRONMENTAL HYSTERICS

In 2008, Maryland governor Martin O'Malley warned that failure to take action on global warming could mean the extinction of the human race. Over the past few years we've been repeatedly warned that we are in the midst of a climate crisis that threatens our survival. Al Gore calls it a "planetary emergency." We might take this concern more seriously if the doom-mongering wing of the environmental movement weren't burdened by a long history of false prophecies.

In the middle to late 1960s, the leading environmental concern was overpopulation. The 1967 book *Famine 1975!* warned "by 1975 a disaster of unprecedented magnitude will face the world...famines will ravage the undeveloped nations...this is the greatest problem facing mankind." A sober review of the book in the scholarly journal *Science* characterized the prediction of mass starvation as "self-evident," argued that technological solutions were "unrealistic," and concluded that catastrophe was unavoidable. The reviewer concluded "all responsible investigators agree that the tragedy will occur."

More widely read was Paul Ehrlich's shrill screed, *The Population Bomb* (1968). Ehrlich began with the infamous words "the battle to feed all of humanity is over," and claimed that "in the 1970s...hundreds of millions of people are going to starve to death." "We must have population control," Ehrlich argued, because it is the "only answer."

Ehrlich followed *The Population Bomb* with publication of an essay titled *Eco-Catastrophe*. In *Eco-Catastrophe* Ehrlich predicted that the Green Revolution would fail and that the "ignorance" of the Cornucopian economists would be exposed. By 1980, environmental degradation would wipe out all "important animal life" in the world's oceans, people would choke to death from air pollution by the hundreds of thousands, and life expectancy in the US would fall to 42 years. "Western society," Ehrlich proclaimed, "is in the process of completing the rape and murder of the planet for economic gain."

In 1975, the news media informed us that a new Ice Age was imminent. An article in the *Chicago Tribune* titled *B-r-r-r: New Ice Age on way soon?*, noted "it's getting colder." The *Tribune* interpreted a number of ordinary weather events "as evidence that a significant shift in climate is taking place--a shift that could be the forerunner of an Ice Age." The *New York Times* chimed in, warning their readers that "a major cooling may be ahead." Famed science reporter Walter Sullivan announced "the world's climate is changing...a new ice age is on the way."

Within ten years, the imminent calamity of global cooling was replaced by global warming. And the mass famines predicted by Paul Ehrlich and others never happened. From 1970 through 2000, the world's population grew from 3.7 billion to 6.1 billion. But the food supply grew faster. Between 1970 and 2000, per capita food increased by 15 percent. The problem today is not one of famine, but of too much food. Obesity is even becoming a problem in the developing world.

Better science and more reasonable voices preceded Ehrlich, but were ignored by a media fascinated with frenetic alarmism. In 1960, ecologist Edward Deevey calmly predicted that the rapid growth in world population would be temporary. He was right. The growth rate of the world population peaked in the early 1960s and was already in decline when Ehrlich published *The Population Bomb* in 1968. Europe and Japan now have negative population growth, and the birth rate in developing countries is falling rapidly as these regions undergo a demographic transition. It is likely that world population will stabilize at 9 to 10 billion around the middle of this century.

None of the environmental catastrophes that Ehrlich predicted occurred. Since 1970, the six principal air pollutants tracked by the EPA have fallen significantly, even while US population and energy use have grown. In 1990, Ehrlich's own ignorance was exposed when he lost a wager over the price of commodities to Cornucopian economist Julian Simon. And the Green Revolution was a success. It has been estimated that the father of the Green Revolution, Norman Borlaug, single-handedly saved the lives of a billion people. Higher crop yields from improved grain varieties also helped preserve the environment by limiting the need to convert undeveloped areas to arable land.

History repeats itself. So, please excuse my skepticism when you claim that global warming means the end of the world is nigh. I have heard it all before.

24 RICE WRONG ON ENERGY

If Oklahomans want to know why gasoline is nearly $4 a gallon, they need to look no farther than the program proposed by Andrew Rice, 2008 candidate for the US Senate. Rice's unimaginative ideas are nothing but a stale imitation of those that have been promoted by the Democratic party in Washington for decades. These ill-advised policies have blocked the development of our native energy resources, resulting in scarcity and high prices.

Rice is opposed to developing America's own petroleum resources by drilling, and has claimed that we should develop "a new energy economy built on renewable natural resources like biomass, switch grass, wind and compressed natural gas." Rice, who holds a Master's Degree in Theology from Harvard, is apparently unaware that natural gas is not a renewable resource, but a fossil fuel.

At a time when oil is scarce and expensive, the most common sense solution imaginable is to drill. But politicians like Rice have placed large parts of our country off-limits for oil exploration and production. Thus we endure the painful and embarrassing spectacle of President Bush begging Saudi Arabia to increase oil production, while awkwardly trying to explain why America refuses to develop its own resources.

We need research into alternative energy. Wind power is a good thing that ought to be developed in Oklahoma. The more energy sources we have in the mix, the better. However, renewable energy sources such as wind, solar, or biofuels are unlikely to make significant contributions to our energy supply for the next several decades. The technologies are not yet sufficiently developed. Wind and solar have low energy densities. They are expensive, intermittent, and incompatible with the existing power grid infrastructure. It is not clear if biofuels deliver more energy than is used in their production.

The non-partisan scientists and analysts at the US Energy Information Administration estimate that by the year 2030, renewable energy sources will barely increase from 5.4 percent of US energy production to 7.6 percent. And much of the present production and anticipated increase is a direct result of legislative mandates, *not* market factors that recognize renewable energy sources as practical, reliable, or inexpensive--the primary attributes of fossil fuels.

The "new economy" that Rice proposes to build on renewable energy is a castle in the air, a foolish fantasy spawned in technological ignorance. Rice apparently does not recognize that limitations to the utilization of renewable energy sources are imposed by the laws of physics and chemistry, not politics. In effect, he proposes to pass legislation that repeals the laws of nature. This is the most embarrassing display of ignorance by a politician since 1897, when the Indiana State Legislature tried to square the circle, a mathematical impossibility.

In both Oklahoma and the US as a whole, we need energy policies that acknowledge the reality that fossil fuels are going to continue to be our primary energy sources for decades to come. Politicians need to stop making scapegoats out of petroleum producers and pass legislation that helps them produce energy. Oklahoma's independent petroleum companies would benefit from research into enhanced-oil-recovery and shale-gas production technologies. These are the sorts of proposals that would actually produce inexpensive energy and bring down the price of gasoline.

25 THE NOBLE SAVAGE

The late Joseph Campbell maintained that civilizations are not based on science, but on myth. "Aspiration," Campbell explained, "is the motivator, builder, and transformer of civilization." Our technological society has been built on Francis Bacon's myth of the New Atlantis.

Competing with Bacon's vision of a scientific society based on intelligence, knowledge, and innovation, is an older, more persistent fable: the Noble Savage. The Noble Savage is not a person, but an idea. It is cultural primitivism, the belief of people living in complex and evolved societies that the simple and primitive life is better. The Noble Savage is the myth that man can live in harmony with nature, that technology is destructive, and that we would all be happier in a more primitive state.

Before Christ lived, the Noble Savage was known to the Hebrews as the Garden of Eden. The Greeks called it the lost Golden Age. In all the ages of the world, otherwise intelligent and learned persons have fallen swoon to the strange appeal of cultural primitivism. In the sixteenth century, French writer Michel de Montaigne described native Americans as so morally pure they had no words in their languages for lying, treachery, avarice, and envy. And Montaigne portrayed the primitive life as so idyllic that American Indians did not have to work, but could spend the whole day dancing.

In 1755, Jean-Jacques Rousseau argued that what appeared to be human progress was in fact decay. The best condition for human beings to live in, according to Rousseau, was the "pure state of nature" in which savages existed. When men lived as hunters and gatherers, they were "free, healthy, honest and happy." The downfall of man occurred when people started to live in cities, acquire private property, and practice agriculture and metallurgy. The acquisition of private property resulted in inequality, aroused the vice of envy, and led to perpetual conflict and unceasing warfare. According to

Rousseau, civilization itself was the scourge of humanity. Rousseau went so far as to make the astonishing claim that the source of all human misery was what he termed our "faculty of improvement," or the use of our minds to improve the human condition.

Since Rousseau wrote, more than two hundred and fifty years of archeological and ethnographic research have shown that most of the imaginative conceptions associated with the Noble Savage are simply wrong. According to archeologist Steven A. Leblanc, "warfare in the past was pervasive and deadly." Conflict between bands of hunter-gatherers was universal and intense, and the practices of cannibalism and infanticide were common. Before the industrial revolution disease and poverty were endemic, even in civilized societies. In eighteenth century Europe half of all children died before their tenth birthday, and life expectancy at birth was only 25 years.

Neither did pre-industrial civilizations live in a state of ecological harmony with their environment. Their exploitation of nature was often destructive. The Mediterranean islands colonized by the ancient Greeks were transformed into barren rock by overgrazing and deforestation. The Bay of Troy, described in Homer's Iliad, has been filled in by sediment eroded from surrounding hillsides destabilized by unsustainable agricultural practices.

All of this would be of academic interest only, were it not the case that the modern environmental movement and many of our public policies are based implicitly on the myth of the Noble Savage. The fountainhead of modern environmentalism is Rachel Carson's *Silent Spring*. The first sentence in *Silent Spring* invoked the Noble Savage by claiming "there was once a town in the heart of America where all life seemed to live in harmony with its surroundings." But the town Carson described did not exist, and her polemic, *Silent Spring*, introduced us to environmental alarmism based on junk science. As the years passed, Rachel Carson was elevated to sainthood and the template laid for endless spasms of hysterical fear-mongering, from the population bomb, to nuclear winter, the Alar scare, and global warming.

The truth is that human beings have not, can not, and never will live in harmony with nature. Our prosperity and health depend on technology driven by energy. We exercise our intelligence to command nature, and were admonished by Francis Bacon to exercise our dominion with "sound reason and true religion." When we are told that our primary energy source, oil, is "making us sick," or that we are "addicted" to oil, these are only the latest examples of otherwise rational persons descending into gibberish after swooning to the lure of the Noble Savage. This ignorant exultation of the primitive can only lead us back to the ages when human lives were "nasty, brutish and short."

26 LIGHT BULB LUNACY

How many persons does it take to change a light bulb? Four hundred, if the people in question are members of the United States Congress. Four hundred is the number of Representatives and Senators who voted in December of 2007 to ban incandescent light bulbs.

Full awareness of this idiocy has not really manifested itself in the public consciousness yet. When it does, there will be an outrage. Beginning in 2012, the manufacture and sale of incandescent light bulbs, starting with the 100-watt bulb, will become illegal. Instead of paying less than twenty cents for a standard incandescent bulb, we will all be forced to purchase compact fluorescent lights (CFLs) for about $3. each or more.

I'm a frugal person. Like other sensible people, I'm interested in saving energy. But I'm skeptical of the exaggerated claims made for CFLs. When these devices were first introduced several years ago, I bought one, anxious to reap the benefits of the claimed energy savings. I was amazed to find that my new 10,000-hour light bulb burned out in a week. The replacement CFL lasted for three months.

Much of the advertising copy we have been sold on CFLs contains exaggerated and misleading claims. The fine print is that the average lifetime is not 10,000 hours, but "up to" 10,000 hours. In many applications, the lifetime of a CFL and estimated energy savings are significantly lower than we have been led to believe. In order for a compact fluorescent bulb to achieve the claimed efficiency, it has to be burned continuously for long periods of time. If a CFL is left on for only five-minute periods of time, it will burn out just as fast as an incandescent bulb. To avoid short cycling, the US Energy Star program advises consumers to leave compact fluorescents on for at least 15 minutes.

This brings up some interesting questions. What procedure should I follow when I have to go into my bedroom closet for 30 seconds? Should I stay in the closet for fifteen minutes, just so the light bulb won't burn out early? Do I have to stay in the bathroom for fifteen minutes every time I go in to pee? What about other lighting applications with short cycles, such as outdoor motion detectors? What are the energy savings, if any, of using CFLs in real-life applications instead of idealized laboratory conditions? What sort of moron mandates that people have to use CFLs in applications they are unsuited for?

It is true that most of the energy utilized by an incandescent bulb goes into heat, not light. But has anyone considered that most of the US is in a temperate climate zone? During a heating month, the heat produced by an incandescent bulb is not wasted, but contributes toward household heating. For most winter months, incandescent bulbs thus achieve an energy efficiency of 100 percent.

There are other problems with CFLs. As most people know, they contain toxic mercury and cannot be thrown into the trash, but have to be recycled. CFLs become dimmer as they age, and thus again will not perform as advertised. The quality of light from fluorescent bulbs is inferior to incandescent. Standard CFLs won't operate at low temperatures and are thus unsuitable for many outdoor applications.

Given that the upcoming ban is on manufacture, not possession or use, it would seem the rational person has only one option: to hoard standard incandescent bulbs while they are still available. Unused light bulbs can be stored indefinitely without degradation. At a unit price of less than 20 cents each, it is eminently practical for most persons to lay in a lifetime supply before the 2012 ban takes effect.

In an ideal world, where the government had some respect for the intelligence of its citizens, consumers would be allowed to make rational decisions about using lighting devices. People would use CFLs in installations they were suited for, indoor applications involving long use cycles. And we would still be allowed to use 100-watt incandescent bulbs in our bedroom closets, where large amounts of light are needed for short periods of time. This is known as free-market economics. During the 20th century it came be recognized as a superior system almost everywhere, even in communist China.

There is one benefit to the light-bulb ban: it serves as a useful voting guide for the upcoming fall elections. In November of 2008, the 86 Senators and 314 Representatives who judged their constituents as not intelligent enough to choose the correct light bulb will undergo a referendum on their own judgment.

27 CALIFORNIA'S CRAZY PLAN

In January of 2007, California was hit by a devastating freeze that caused more than a billion dollars of damage. Crops were destroyed, produce prices soared, and agricultural workers lost their jobs. California's response to this disaster is to adopt a bold and ludicrous plan to fight global warming. If the plan works, two hundred years of human progress will be reversed. More orchards will be frozen, California's economy will be crippled, and people's electric bills will skyrocket.

Our preoccupation with global warming is reminiscent with the medieval obsession with demons. Both are omnipresent, yet unseen and undetectable. Global warming is most commonly defined as the dramatic temperature increase projected by computer models a hundred years hence. Left unsaid is the fact that these imaginative models have never been tested. The models are speculative, and rely upon an assumption that water vapor will magnify the putative warming effect of carbon dioxide through positive feedback. But it may well be that water vapor will exert a negative feedback and cool the Earth through cloud formation.

If you demonstrate that you're astute enough to understand the Achille's Heel of the models, then the alarmists will define global warming as the modest temperature increase, less than one degree Celsius, that has taken place over the last 150 years. But if you point out that the instrumental record is contaminated by the urban heat island effect, then global warming becomes the greenhouse effect, something that can be demonstrated in the laboratory and is therefore irrefutable. However most heat transfer in the atmosphere is convective, not radiative. The complexities of heat transfer in the atmosphere cannot be replicated in either the laboratory or by a computer model. When subjected to critical scrutiny by an informed and intelligent person, every argument for the existence of global warming fails.

Only the ignorant believe in global warming. This little demon can only exist in the dark, and he can easily be erased by the plain light of factual evidence. The mean planetary temperature, as determined by satellite measurements, was the same in 2008 as it was in 1980. The extent of global sea ice was also the same as it was in 1980. Cyclone and hurricane activity in the northern hemisphere was at a 24-year low. Consider this anecdote. On December 14, 2008, the temperature in Denver fell to minus 15 degrees Fahrenheit, breaking the old record of minus 14 Fahrenheit set in 1901. If global warming is real, is it not remarkable that such a thing happened?

Suppose we grant the implausible assumption that carbon dioxide will dramatically warm our planet as predicted by the computer models. We might then ask, what will be the cooling effect of reducing carbon dioxide emissions? What is the benefit of forcing people to replace inexpensive, reliable, and abundant carbon fuels, with 13th-century windmills, inefficient and expensive solar cells, and other unreliable power sources? The amazing answer is that there will no benefit whatsoever.

One reason the US rejected the Kyoto Treaty was a calculation showing that even if fully implemented, it would only reduce planetary temperature by about one-tenth of a degree Celsius by the year 2100. Bjorn Lomborg has recently pointed out that Britain's hideously expensive plan to force renewable energy down people's throats may eventually reduce Earth's temperature by the remarkable amount of one three-thousandth of a degree-- at most. Let us generously assume that California's plan can be successfully implemented and has ten times the effect of the British effort. Do Californians really understand that the best possible result from having their electric bills tripled is the possibility that the temperature might be reduced by one three-hundreths of a degree at some imaginary point in a far distant future?

It is apparent that a significant portion of our population is lost in an irrational moral and religious frenzy. Their goal appears to be nothing less than to reverse the industrial revolution and force us all back to the days when human lives were "nasty, brutish and short." This is not science; it is superstition. You won't like the result.

28 WATER WOES OVERSTATED

According to a 2010 report by the Environmental Working Group, drinking water in Norman, Oklahoma, contains the highest level of chromium 6 in the US, 12.9 parts per billion. Chromium 6 is a known carcinogen, but its relatively high level in Norman city water is unlikely to be a health problem.

Toxicity depends on dosage. Any substance--even distilled water--is potentially toxic when consumed in large quantities. In 2007, a twenty-eight-year-old woman died of water intoxication after drinking too much bottled water. Selenium is a trace element that is known to be highly toxic. In 2006, an Australian man perished only six hours after consuming a mere ten grams of sodium selenite. But sodium selenite is also an essential nutrient that is sold as a dietary supplement in health food stores. People add small amounts of selenium to their diets because there is significant scientific evidence that ingestion of optimal amounts of this mineral reduces the incidence of cancer in animals. Substances that are toxic in large amounts can be beneficial and even essential when consumed in small amounts.

In the human body, chromium 6 is converted to the more common form of chromium 3 and vice versa. Chromium 3 is found in common foods such as bread, milk, and vegetables. People in the US daily obtain about a tenth of a milligram of chromium 3 in their diets. Chromium in involved in insulin metabolism, and it has been hypothesized that insufficient dietary intake of chromium 3 may contribute to the development of diabetes.

The primary evidence that chromium 6 causes cancer in humans is an epidemiological study from China where water was contaminated with chromium 6 levels up to 1550 times higher than the levels found in Norman city water. These high levels of chromium 6 were correlated with an increased incidence of stomach cancer. If chromium 6 in Norman water caused cancer, the stomach cancer rate in Cleveland County would be above average. But it is below average. Between 2003 and 2007, deaths from stomach cancer in Cleveland County were 2.7 per 100,000 population, twenty-nine percent lower than the US average of 3.7 per 100,000.

The mere fact that chromium 6 is a carcinogen should not be alarming. Carcinogens are not limited to environmental contaminants such as chromium 6. Many natural foods contain carcinogens. These include beer (ethyl alcohol), apples (caffeic acid), and peanut butter (aflatoxin). Coffee contains more than a thousand chemicals, half of which are carcinogenic. Trace amounts of carcinogenic substances do not commonly cause cancer because the human body contains defense enzymes that are effective against both natural and synthetic carcinogens.

When we exaggerate exotic risks, we divert attention and resources from common factors that are much more likely to cause premature death. The leading causes of premature morbidity are smoking, physical inactivity, poor diet, and automobile accidents. These are all preventable. We would all live longer and be healthier if we just applied some common sense, drove defensively, and took better care of our bodies.

29 NATIONAL HEALTH CARE: THE LAST THING WE NEED

Suppose I were a salesman from a hypothetical insurance company and knocked on your door one day to offer you a health insurance policy with the following terms and conditions.

Once you join our system, you will never be able to leave. Premiums will be deducted from your paycheck whether you like it or not and may be increased at any time without your consent.

You will be placed in the same group with high-risk individuals. These will include intravenous drug users at risk for AIDS, cigarette smokers and the overweight and sedentary. You will have to bear the financial responsibility for their irresponsible lifestyle.

We can change the amount and extent of your coverage at any time we want without your consent. There are no guarantees you can choose your own doctor, receive the treatment your doctor recommends, or even be able to see a doctor at all. All these decisions will be made for you.

We have a very poor record of financial responsibility. For example, we have a retirement system that may not be able to pay retirement benefits for the people who are currently contributing to it because we are siphoning off money to pay our other debts. In fact, our company has been bankrupt for more than thirty years and grows deeper in debt every day. The only way we can stay in business is by borrowing money to pay interest on the money we already own.

We cannot be sued and are immune from criminal prosecution. However, if you break our rules we can arrest and imprison you. Of course, none of these rules pertain to the executives of our company.

Doesn't sound like a deal that anyone in his right mind would make, does it? Yet this is the insurance plan that proponents of national health insurance want us to join. Instead of being free to spend our money on any one of the hundreds of private insurance plans that are currently available, under national health insurance we would be forced to join a plan run by the federal government--the most wasteful, inefficient and poorly run organization in the country.

If national health insurance is such a good thing, is participation going to be voluntary? Of course not. No one would join, because a government plan could never compete with private insurance. Government does not function as efficiently as private industry because government bureaucracies are accountable to no one, do not have to compete with anyone and have no incentive to produce quality service.

A good example of the failure of national health care is provided by our neighbors in Canada. Canadian patients commonly have to wait months or years for elective surgery. The waiting period for necessary and even emergency surgery may be months. Because of this, many Canadians carry private insurance policies and end up going to the US for treatment.

If a person is given a choice between (a) spending their own money on health care as they see fit, or (b) handing it over to a third party who will spend it for them after subtracting a percentage, only an irrational person will choose to let someone else spend their money. Yet this is exactly what national health insurance is all about.

The reason people want it is that they have been misled into thinking that they aren't going to have to pay for their own health insurance--government will pay for it. However, the only money government has is the money it forcibly collects from us and our neighbors through taxation. We can't all get rich through this redistribution of wealth, we can only lose our freedom.

There is no denying, however, that healthcare is unreasonably expensive. Why? Because government interference has destroyed the free market in health care.

The primary health care providers in this country, physicians, have been given a monopoly by the government. According to US Bureau of Labor Statistics, the average annual salary for physicians in the US as of 2010 was in the neighborhood of $200,000.

As highly skilled professionals who must complete years of training, physicians ought to be able to earn high salaries. But this level of compensation could not be sustained in a free market. Because physicians make such high salaries, many people should be attracted to the medical profession. The number of physicians would increase and competition would drive down the cost of their services.

However, the normal rules of supply and demand do not operate because of government interference. State medical licensing boards restrict the number of schools who can train physicians and number of people granted licenses to practice. Physicians have no competition, and the patient has no choice--pay up or die. No one else can provide you with health care because they would be arrested and thrown in prison.

Another area in which government interference has driven up the cost of health care is in the regulation of pharmaceuticals by the Food and Drug Administration (FDA). No drug can be marketed unless it is proven to be safe and effective. Sounds like a good idea, doesn't it? However, not only does this difficult process keep many worthwhile drugs off the market, it also adds to their expense. And many drugs that were deemed "safe and effective" by the FDA were later discovered to be dangerous and ineffective.

But wouldn't unscrupulous drug companies take advantage of people if we did away with this requirement? Perhaps, but it is in a company's own self-interest to produce quality products. Product liability lawsuits would quickly bankrupt a dishonest pharmaceutical manufacturer. If the FDA certification process were optional, consumers would then have a choice between FDA certified and non-certified products.

Restoring health care to a free market system in this country would provide the greatest access to the best health care by the largest number of people. A practical solution would be to institute a tier of health care professionals. The state could set standards and charge modest licensing fees.

Of course, obtaining a license of any type would be optional. Individuals would then be free to choose between licensed and unlicensed health care providers. Competition between different types of health care providers would result in increased efficiency and productivity. Costs would come down as health care products and services adjust to free market conditions.

Physicians would probably be at the top of the tier of health care professionals and offer the most expensive health care. Those not willing or able to pay for the services of a physician could hire a nurse practitioner or health care technician. Other specialists such as chiropractors, respiratory therapists and midwives would also be able to practice their professions without fear of prosecution. Under this system you would be empowered to make decisions about your own body, not some government bureaucrat.

Wouldn't the quality of care suffer? I don't think so. A nurse practitioner or health technician would likely refer cases beyond their capability to physicians or face lawsuits for medical malpractice. A good example of health care providers who currently function in this respect is chiropractors. They routinely refer problems beyond their expertise to physicians. The quality of health care would probably improve. Routine problems such as the common cold could be handled by health care technicians, freeing physicians to devote more time to care of the truly ill.

In summary, the last thing we need in this country is another government bureaucracy to run our lives and take away more of our vanishing freedom. Most problems with the health care system today are due to government interference in the free market. Restoring a free market in health care is the best way to provide health care for the least amount of money to the most people.

30 MEN AND WOMEN ARE NOT CREATED EQUAL

Some people have complained that female enrollment in the College of Engineering at the University of Oklahoma is too low because 80 percent of engineering students at OU are men. This inequality has been attributed to sociological factors such as a lack of role models and traditional attitudes. However, there are also important biological differences between the sexes that may contribute to men's tendency to favor engineering.

There are differences in the average levels of cognitive abilities between men and women, and these differences can influence career decisions. On average, females have better verbal abilities than males. Males, however, tend to be superior in visual-spatial skills and mathematics, both of which may be important in engineering.

Contrary to popular opinion, there is virtual unanimity in the psychological sciences that these differences exist. For example, a study by C. P. Benbow and J. C. Stanley that was published in *Science* in 1980 documented "huge sex differences...in mathematical aptitude...in favor of boys." The authors concluded that the most likely explanation for the differences they found was "superior male mathematical ability."

There is significant scientific evidence that sex-based differences in spatial and mathematical abilities may be biological in origin. For example, a study by K. T. and K. G. Hoyenga showed that male rats are better at navigating mazes than females. I concede it is possible that those female rats performed poorly because they were distressed by the lack of proper role models, but somehow this seems implausible.

Are the people who present themselves as being concerned about gender equity sincere? Consider that any inequality which may accrue to the advantage of men is presented as a profound sociological problem, while those inequalities which work against men are ignored.

Consider enrollment in nursing. When I called the OU College of Nursing in Oklahoma City, I was told that men make up only 14 percent of undergraduate nursing majors. Why isn't anyone upset about this?

If we are going to have true equality between the sexes, then we ought to address the critical problem of prison populations. Approximately 94 percent of all prisoners in the United States are male. If gender equity is desirable in engineering enrollment, why not in prison population? Should we increase parole opportunities for male prisoners and pursue the prosecution of females more vigorously? Or should we continue to treat each criminal as an individual, judged on the basis of his or her actions?

I know this may come as a shock to many of you, but it is a fact that there are profound physiological differences between men and women. When people with different abilities and inclinations make decisions in a free society, inequalities result.

Equality in opportunities is desirable, but it does not necessarily lead to equality in outcomes.

31 GENDER INEQUALITIES AND INEQUITIES

Western Civilization has a long history of patriarchy. Male superiority was an unquestioned cultural norm in ancient Greece and Rome. Women were considered to be property. Solon (c. 638-558 BC) had to pass a law forbidding men from selling daughters or wives into slavery. In *The Republic*, Plato sarcastically noted that women were only superior in the "management of pancakes and preserves." Aristotle concluded explicitly that "the male is by nature superior," and infamously noted that "silence is a woman's glory."

In 195 BC, Cato the Censor complained about Roman women having the audacity to petition the Senate for repeal of the Oppian Law. He noted, "our ancestors thought it proper that women should ever be under the control of parents, brothers, or husbands." Near the end of the first century AD in Rome, the poet Juvenal wrote *The Ways of Women*, a catalog of female vices. Women were shameless harlots. They were cruel, cowardly, and disputatious. The most intolerable of all females was one with a pretension to learning.

The advent of Christianity brought little relief. Eve committed the greatest crime of all time when she picked the forbidden fruit and corrupted Adam. Henceforth women were condemned to be ruled by their husbands (*Genesis* 3.16). The Apostle Paul characterized women as spiritually inferior to men. Women were not allowed to speak in church meetings, and were advised to submit to their husbands.

In medieval Europe, women were invariably prosecuted for witchcraft more often than men. The authors of the *Malleus Maleficarum*, a handbook for the prosecution of witches, argued that the prevalence of witchcraft among women was a fact. "A greater number of witches is found in the fragile feminine sex than among men; it is indeed a fact that it were idle to contradict." Women were characterized as "unescapable punishments, necessary evils, natural temptations, desirable calamities, and domestic dangers."

In the US, women did not obtain the right to vote until 1920. Through the 1960s, the proper role for a woman was considered to be a mother and homemaker.

Times have changed. There is no institutional or private employer in the US today that openly discriminates against women. Barriers have been removed, but inequalities remain. Men continue to dominate areas such as engineering and the physical sciences.

The stubborn persistence of inequalities in these professions has been explained by a fashionable aggregate of dogmatic beliefs. Male domination is invariably attributed to hostile climates, negative stereotypes, and imperceptible but all-encompassing societal biases. All of these explanations are invisible, undetectable, and therefore irrefutable. Implicit is the belief that human biology is infinitely malleable and that there are no inherent sex-based differences in abilities and inclinations--a view that is contrary to all scientific research and human knowledge.

The process of educational and professional training is claimed to be analogous to a "pipeline" instead of a sorting operation. Women have to be pushed through the pipeline even if it runs contrary to their natural inclinations and temperaments. The nebulous concept of Diversity is invoked as sort of a pagan idol that we are supposed to worship without question.

In response to tenacious inequalities, institutions have adopted explicit hiring biases wherein strong preferences are given to female candidates. Bias and discrimination are known by the euphemism of "affirmative action." The announcement of nearly every job opportunity in academia is followed by the oxymoronic notice that the institution is both an "affirmative action" and an "equal opportunity" employer. In academic and professional circles, the bias against men has evolved within a few short decades into a universally accepted cultural norm.

The old generation of principled feminists who fought for equal opportunity has been replaced by a new cadre of shrill, neurotic harpies that demand preferential treatment. These self-serving opportunists characterize every inequality that works to the disadvantage of women as an inequity, but are oblivious to the advantages that US women enjoy.

Women in US colleges receive better grades than men and are more likely to graduate. On average, US women live five years longer than men, and therefore receive five additional years of Social Security payments. Wouldn't it be fairer if the retirement age for men was five years earlier than for women? Ninety-three percent of all people incarcerated in US prisons are men. If equity is synonymous with numerical equality, then why don't we start paroling men earlier and begin prosecuting women more vigorously?

Today's feminist society is disgusting and hypocritical. I prefer the honest biases of the nineteenth century. Men denied opportunities to women, but not out of selfish motives. Women were discriminated against because of deeply but honestly held cultural values. No one had the effrontery to describe discrimination as "equal opportunity."

The nineteenth-century German philosopher Nietzsche said that there was no point in men trying to grant equality to women because women will never be satisfied with mere equality. The war between the sexes is eternal. Peace can only come with victory and the total subordination of men. The present generation of feminists appears to be proving him correct.

32 SOCIALISM'S DARK ROOTS

Modern American political philosophies have their roots in the eighteenth-century philosophical movement known as the Enlightenment. In *Common Sense*, the most influential pamphlet of the American Revolution, Thomas Paine characterized government as a "necessary evil," and argued for freedom from arbitrary and tyrannical rule. Paine's philosophy of individual freedom and limited government influenced the formulation of the US Constitution and Bill of Rights. The experiment was a success. Never in the history of the world has a country enjoyed more political freedom or material prosperity than the United States.

But the Enlightenment produced a dark offspring, socialism. In socialism, the paramount duty of government is not to secure the political and economic freedom of citizens, but to form the character of individuals through education. Because a person's character is the result of their early education, a process over which they have no control, socialists believe that people are not responsible for their own actions and have to be controlled by government.

The father of socialism was the Welsh reformer, Robert Owen (1771-1858). In 1825, Owen put his theories to the test by forming a utopian socialistic community in Indiana named New Harmony. The experiment went badly. Instead of forming a cohesive, egalitarian society, the residents of New Harmony aggregated into cliques based on education or class. In 1826, Owen claimed that the sources of all "ignorance, poverty, and vice" in the world were private property, traditional religion, and marriage. Owen's intellectual heirs have worked for nearly two hundred years to eradicate these institutions from our society.

New Harmony failed miserably. In the space of a little more than two years, Owen was forced to reorganize the community no less than ten times.

By March of 1827, there were so few people left in New Harmony that Owen was forced to admit defeat. But rather than take responsibility and concede the fault lay in his own ideas, Owen blamed the failure on the inhabitants of his utopian society. New Harmony wasn't the only debacle. Without exception, every single attempt to put Owen's socialistic ideas into practice failed. By 1830, the total number of failed experiments was nineteen.

After nineteen failed tests, a sane person might have been forced to the conclusion that the fundamental problem lay in their basic thesis. Not Robert Owen. To the end of his life, Owen remained entirely oblivious to Aristotle's dictum that political science must deal with people as they are, not as theoreticians wished them to be. In 1847, Owen published a tract where he complained that people who resisted indoctrination in socialism were mentally ill. Owen concluded that he was the only sane person in the world.

Sadly, people learned nothing from Owen's failures. His socialism matured into communism. During the twentieth century, communist governments were directly responsible for the death of a hundred million people. Bad ideas and ignorance of history can be costly.

In the United States today, we are largely oblivious to the fact that every good thing in our society springs from our heritage of individual freedom and limited government. None dare speak the truth. Socialism is not dead, it has merely been renamed liberalism. Liberal politicians in America today work tirelessly to enlarge government, divide people, and take away freedoms. If they had their way, these irrational control freaks would micromanage every detail of our personal lives.

Toward the end of his life Robert Owen became a spiritualist, a person who believes the living can communicate with the dead. That seems fitting, because liberals today continue to communicate the dead idea of socialism to the living.

33 WHY OBAMA WILL LOSE

When Benjamin Franklin was dispatched to France as ambassador of the United States in 1776, he won the hearts of the French through his authenticity. Rather than take on an affected and phony continental style, Franklin eschewed the powdered wig of the european gentleman and donned the fur cap of an American frontiersman. Original genius and polymath, Franklin understood that the French would see through any false pretension but respect an authenticity that sprang from an unpretentious and naive love of country.

What a contrast there is between Franklin and Barack Hussein Obama. Obama is a Harvard lawyer, whose most significant accomplishment in life is being educated beyond the level of his intelligence. A mile wide and an inch deep, Obama is only the latest in a long line of shallow elites that consider it stylish and intellectual to despise their own culture and heritage.

Nothing exemplifies Obama's antipathy for American culture better than his statement that Americans "cling to" religion and guns out of frustration or bitterness. We can only suppose that Mr. Obama regards religion or firearms as aberrations that need to be eradicated. In an Obama administration, the people who "cling" to them will presumably be interred in Soviet-style gulags where they can be medicated and receive systematic instruction in the principles of correct thinking.

Of course, both guns and religion are essential aspects of American culture. The United States was founded by people seeking religious freedom. Does the word "Pilgrim" ring a bell with anyone? Our freedom and the right to self-government were won by farmers with guns. The American Revolution started when the British marched to Concord with the intention of confiscating colonial arms. Both the right to "keep and bear arms," and the right to "free exercise" of religion are enshrined in the Bill of Rights. We have come a long way when the presidential nominee of a major political party regards the exercise of fundamental rights as a mental aberration.

When Obama refers to "my Muslim faith," the verbal gaffe resonates as a Freudian slip because of Obama's thinly veiled hatred for this country's unique culture and institutions. Obama sat for twenty years in a church where the Rev. Jeremiah Wright Jr., preached "goddamn America." He only resigned from the congregation when it became politically expedient to do so. When earlier this year, Michelle Obama said "for the first time in my adult life, I am proud of my country," can we conclude that her husband disagrees? Is it not remarkable that Mrs. Obama can be so small-minded as to find *nothing* in the history of the United States that merits her admiration but the personal success of her husband?

What is Mr. Obama *for*? His campaign motto is "change." But even a six-year-old child understands that "change" can be either good or bad. Lacking specifics, the invocation of "change" as policy is completely empty. As we witness Obama's minions mindlessly endorse the meaningless maxim of "change," it can only call to mind the barnyard animals in George Orwell's *Animal Farm* chanting "four legs good, two legs bad!"

The choice of Sarah Palin as John McCain's running mate has been devastating for the Obama campaign precisely because she is everything Obama is not. Palin is not ashamed of her culture or country. She is not embarrassed by being an American, but naively embraces her birthright. Unassisted by affirmative action, Governor Palin has risen to national prominence on the basis of her character, intelligence, and natural gifts. In word, she has guts. This is a woman who is proud of her country, not because it has granted her personal success, but because she respects what America stands for: freedom, opportunity, and individualism.

Barack Obama is a vapid demagogue, a hollow man that despises American culture. He is ill-suited to be President of the United States, but well-qualified to be the dictator of a socialist state like Cuba. As the weeks pass, more Americans will come to this realization and elect McCain/Palin in a landslide.

34 WRONG ABOUT OBAMA

A little more than three years ago, I predicted that Obama would lose the 2008 presidential election. I was wrong. I failed to foresee the economic crisis that developed in September of 2008. The electorate would have voted for any Democrat running that year. It didn't help that the Republican nominee, John McCain, came across as wooden, inarticulate, and out-of-touch. Republicans have a way of snatching defeat from the jaws of victory.

But time has proven me right about the larger issues. Obama is a socialist and a vapid demagogue who has been educated beyond the level of his intelligence. He is the choice of a puerile and spoiled electorate who want to be taken care of and obtain handouts from a parental figurehead.

I can't believe the West won the Cold War. The Cold War was a competition of economic ideologies. In the 1960s, we used to have sincere debates about which economic system was better, a socialist, centrally-planned economy, or a capitalist, free-market economy. The debate is over. By 1990, even the Russians and Chinese were forced to implicitly admit the superiority of market economies. But while our former enemies were busy converting their socialist systems to market economies, we were happily rushing headlong into socialism.

People have been discussing economic systems for more than two thousand years. As described in my books, *Science and Technology in World History, Vols. 1 & 2,* communism was advocated by Plato as early as the fourth century BC. But Plato's student, Aristotle, disparaged communism by observing "that which is common to the greatest number has the least care bestowed upon it. Every one thinks chiefly of his own, hardly at all of the common interest; and only when he is himself concerned as an individual." Aristotle concluded that the ills which are supposed to arise from private property in fact originated in human nature.

We have been aware of the superiority of market economies since Adam Smith published *Wealth of Nations* in 1776. When a person is left free to pursue their own interest unimpeded he is "led by an invisible hand to promote an end which was no part of his intention...[and thus] by pursuing his own interest he frequently promotes that of society more effectually than when he really intends to promote it."

In *Principles of Political Economy* (1848), John Stuart Mill (1806-1873) gave three reasons to severely limit government interference in a nation's economy and markets. First, any increase in government power is a threat to human individuality, freedom, and originality, qualities necessary for the progress of the human race. Second, market economies function more efficiently and produce more prosperity. Third, laissez faire economies inculcate moral virtues in citizens by making them more self-reliant, virtuous and intelligent. "A people," Mill explained, "who expect to have everything done for them...have their faculties only half developed."

The test of any theory is experiment, but it is virtually impossible to conduct large-scale controlled experiments in economics. It is even difficult to even make meaningful and unambiguous comparisons between countries. Nations differ, not only in economic systems, but in cultures, languages, traditions, geographies, and natural resources. To test socialism versus capitalism we would have to take one or more countries with similar social and physical characteristics and divide them in half. After assigning a different economic system to each country, we would then sit back for fifty years and observe what happens.

But this experiment has already been performed through an accident of history. *We know the answer.* At the close of World War II, Germany and Korea were divided into socialist and market economies. Socialism failed dramatically. East Germany had to build the Berlin Wall just to keep people from fleeing. North Korea is still in the stone age. A satellite photo taken at night shows South Korea ablaze with the light of civilization. But North Korea is dark, both literally and metaphorically.

In the US, we exist in a curious state of denial. We acknowledge the inferiority of socialism, but continue to become more and more socialistic. Every attempt to shrink the size of government or repeal a regulation brings about a shriek, like a bottle being pulled out of the mouth of an infant. I cannot recall a Republican President or Congress that reduced the size of the Federal government. No one wants to surrender their special privilege or entitlement. We know what the best system is, but lack the discipline to return to it.

Ronald Reagan used to say that liberals only know how to tax and spend. If there was ever a man who embodies that aphorism, it is Barack Obama. He has no clue as to how a free market economy works or why it produces economic prosperity. Obama continues to insist that government should determine what energy technologies we're going to have. Thus the debacle of Solyndra. Five hundred million dollars went down the drain needlessly. Government can't pick winners because it doesn't know how to do so. If a centrally-planned socialist system worked, it would have produced prosperity in China, the Soviet Union, and North Korea. It didn't. Only a free market system knows how to efficiently distribute resources.

Since the inception of Lyndon Johnson's "Great Society," we have had at least forty years of welfare programs designed to reduce poverty. These programs have not worked. The current US poverty rate is the same that it was in the late 1960s. So what do we do about it? Instead of reversing course, we continue on the same path. If the "Occupy Wall St." protestors have no jobs, it is because they are reaping the rewards of their own success. Socialism has killed the prosperity produced by our formerly great system. The US is now ninth on the index of economic freedom and heading downward.

Yes, we have a clueless idiot for President. But we have no one but ourselves to blame. Obama was chosen by the people of the US. He was elected democratically, and therefore is nothing more than an iconic representation of our own ignorance, greed, and infantile sense of entitlement. Obama is not the problem, and his electoral defeat in 2012 will not magically heal the country or return us to prosperity and freedom.

Elections change nothing, because they are not causes but results. The US Congress now has an all-time low approval rating of nine percent. This is nothing more than an indication that we have lost the ability to govern ourselves. After all, we elect our Congressional representatives. We have the government we deserve. Prosperity and freedom will only return if and when the American people again become educated, virtuous, and intelligent.

35 AMERICANS ARE FAT, LAZY AND STUPID

Who's responsible for the financial meltdown of 2008? Those blamed include President Bush, Wall Street, and Congress. But in truth, the American people have no one to blame but themselves. The United States was founded by people who wanted nothing more than freedom and the opportunity to work toward a better life for their children. But within a few generations, the progeny of the pioneers have turned into dolts who can't take responsibility for anything.

When I say that Americans are fat, I'm not speaking metaphorically, but literally. About one-third of adults in the US are obese. To qualify as "obese," the average person has to be not just overweight, but carry an extra thirty-five pounds or more. In the last thirty years, the obesity rate in America has more than doubled. It is the sheerest irony that today the average person has the choice of a multiplicity of fresh, wholesome, and nutritious foods, all available at the lowest prices in history. But choosing and preparing the best foods takes time and effort. We would rather stuff ourselves with fast food, because it's tasty and convenient. The consequences of this slothful lifestyle include hypertension, diabetes, and heart disease. After ruining our health through gluttony, we then go to our physicians and demand a quick fix in the form of a pill. Pharmaceutical companies are glad to oblige. And the government must pay, because free health care is now a "right."

Stupid? The average American spends three hours a day watching television. What started out fifty years ago as simple entertainment has turned into an open running sewer. The television networks are locked in a downward spiral to see who can provide the most outrageous and offensive programming. It's not their fault. They're just giving the American people what they want. I'm always amazed to hear parents express the morbid fear that their children will become involved with drugs, when in fact their children are already addicted to television. The average child today spends thirteen hours watching television for every hour they spend reading. We blame teachers and schools for failing to educate our children, but there is little that can be done with minds that expect to be entertained and rebel at the labor of thought.

We are adept at prideful self-congratulation, but oblivious to the fact that our society is intellectually and artistically bankrupt. Modern art is not good enough to be bad, and popular music is a painful cacophony of obnoxious dissonance. The internet is mostly used for downloading pornography or playing video games. We are obsessed with watching people we have never met play games with footballs, basketballs, and baseballs. I am baffled by what people find so fascinating about these meaningless games.

In America today, everyone is entitled to everything. The financial crisis was caused by politicians pressuring financial institutions to give mortgages to people who were poor credit risks. But the politicians simply did what the voters wanted. Americans have been blessed with the greatest freedoms and opportunities in the world. But we have incessantly demanded more and more entitlements and handouts. Every government intervention in the free market system creates a fresh problem that demands another ruinous intervention with unintended consequences.

In this brave new world, everyone has the right to not be offended, and no one can be held accountable for anything. The divorce rate is fifty percent. The number of Americans with AIDS is a million and growing. In the six years between 2000 and 2006, the syphilis infection rate doubled. The nation that began with freedom of religion has progressed to freedom from religion, freedom from moral constraint, and freedom from responsibility. Just as Plato described in the *Republic*, the "horses and asses" are "marching along with all the rights and dignities of freemen," and the ultimate result can only be that "tyranny will spring from democracy."

No matter who wins the presidential election in November of 2008, the outcome will be the same. There will be a brief period of euphoria, followed by an inevitable course of disenchantment. The President of the United States is a weak constitutional officer, not a god or a parent. He can't solve problems that are rooted in our behaviors. So long as Americans look to other people for the solution of their problems, they will invariably be disappointed. The American people need to stop whining like spoiled children and take charge of their lives.

36 AMERICA IS GONE

There is a whiff of anarchy in the air this morning. As I sit here writing, a conservative victory in the 2010 midterm elections looms. But I find no reason to be optimistic. The midterm elections will solve nothing. The plain fact is that conservatives have lost the battle for America. The country that many of us were born in has ceased to exist. And we have no one to blame but ourselves. Nothing can or will change until we come to terms with the grim reality of moral degeneration. And I have no hopes that this can happen, save by some terrible trial.

Last week in Oklahoma City two pedestrians were run down by cars at the same intersection within a few hours. In one incident, the driver did not bother to stop, but continued driving on as if nothing had happened. It was a horrific but perfect metaphor for the self-absorbed entitlement mentality that grips the country.

Every day the news brings a startling new incident of moral corruption. A few days ago it was reported that an eighteen-year-old geology student at Arizona State University had starred in an online pornographic film in which she performed "explicit and degrading" sex acts for a one-time payment of $2000. The young woman explained that she needed the money to supplement her scholarship, and then inexplicably proclaimed, "I have morals!"

We are a nation of gluttons. About one-third of adults in the US are obese. To qualify as "obese," the average person has to be not just overweight, but carry an extra thirty-five pounds or more. In the last thirty years, the obesity rate in America has more than doubled. It is the sheerest irony that today the average person has the choice of a multiplicity of fresh, wholesome, and nutritious foods, all available at the lowest prices in history. But choosing and preparing the best foods takes time and effort. We would rather stuff ourselves with fast food, because it's tasty and convenient. The consequences of this slothful lifestyle include hypertension, diabetes, and heart disease. After ruining our health through gluttony, we then go to our physicians and demand a quick fix in the form of a pill. Pharmaceutical companies are glad to oblige. And the government must pay, because free health care is now a "right."

There is no better index for America's moral degradation than television programming. Compare today's shows with those of a generation ago. Every episode of the *Andy Griffith* program contained a short moral lesson, and the *Twilight Zone* challenged our intellects and stretched our imaginations. But entertainment and instruction have devolved into shock and novelty. The networks are locked in a downward spiral to see who can provide the most outrageous and offensive programming. It's not their fault. They're just giving the American people what they want.

Children are not as smart as their parents. The average child today spends thirteen hours watching television for every hour they spend reading. We blame teachers and schools for failing to educate our children. But what can they do with undeveloped and undisciplined minds that expect to be entertained and rebel at the labor of thought? The decline in intellectual aptitude is so dramatic that the authors of the SAT test have had to add 100 points to the combined math and verbal score just to make current averages equal of those of a generation ago.

We are oblivious to the fact that our society is intellectually and artistically bankrupt. Modern art is not good enough to be bad. At the beginning of the sixteenth century, Leonardo da Vinci took four years to paint *Mona Lisa*. He left the work unfinished, because Leonardo was always seeking to add "perfection to perfection." Earlier this year, x-ray fluorescence spectroscopy revealed that the way Leonardo created realistic flesh tones was by building up successive layers of pigments that were as thin as a few micrometers. A micrometer is a *thousandth* of a millimeter.

Compare Leonardo's work with that of the modern American artist, Robert Ryman. Ryman began his career working as a security guard at a museum. The guard decided he wanted to become a painter so he bought some white house paint and slathered it on a canvas. Art critics had orgasms. For decades, Ryman has continued to produced paintings that consist of nothing but monochrome white. The tones and textures vary, but most of Ryman's paintings consist of nothing but a plain white surface. Ryman has explained that he paints only white surfaces because he wants to "reduce visual disturbances." Imagine that the next time you're contemplating Michelangelo's "disturbances" on the ceiling of the Sistine Chapel.

Our popular music is a painful cacophony of obnoxious dissonance. The eighteenth and nineteenth centuries had Mozart, Beethoven, and Tchaikovsky. We have Snoop Dogg and Lady Gaga. Is that progress? We have advanced technology, but do we use it uplift ourselves? No, we indulge the animal side of our natures. The internet is mostly used for downloading pornography or playing video games.

In America today, everyone is entitled to everything. According to a recent report by NPR, the mentally retarded are now attending college and receiving grants. Professors are being advised (i.e., pressured) to modify their curricula to accommodate the new students. People incessantly demand entitlements and handouts. Every government intervention in the free market system creates a fresh problem that demands another ruinous intervention with unintended consequences. Nobody is responsible for anything, and no one wants to pay the bills. And believe me, they're coming due.

In this brave new world, everyone has the right to not be offended, and no one can be held accountable for anything. The fundamental unit of human civilization, the family, has been caustically eroded by feminism. The divorce rate is fifty percent. Oklahoma is supposedly a conservative state. Last year, a state legislator introduced a bill that would require parents with minor children seeking a divorce to first undergo counseling. Not only was the bill not passed, the legislator was derided and mocked. How dare anyone be required to undertake the work necessary to save a marriage for the sake of their children? Why, it might interfere with their pursuit of happiness.

We celebrate homosexuality, and then wonder why sexually transmitted diseases are exploding. According to the CDC, men-who-have-sex-with-men make up only two percent of the population, but account for 53 percent of all new HIV infections and 64 percent of all new syphilis cases.

I'm beginning to acquire an appreciation for Paul's doctrine of Original Sin. The nation that began with freedom of religion has progressed to freedom from religion, freedom from moral constraint, and freedom from responsibility. Just as Plato described in the *Republic*, the "horses and asses" are "marching along with all the rights and dignities of freemen," and the ultimate result can only be that "tyranny will spring from democracy."

Elections only matter in the short term. Every long term social index I am aware of is negative. The plain fact is that the American people are too morally degenerate to be capable of effective self government. The Roman satirist Juvenal understood. "The people that once bestowed commands, consulships, legions and all else, now meddles no more and longs eagerly for just two things--bread and games!" I can find no reason to be optimistic. It is only our blind vanity that lets us pretend that the United States can endure forever. Rome fell, and so will America. For all intents and purposes, it is already over.

37 DECLINE OF THE AMERICAN COMIC BOOK

May 3 , 2003, was "free comic book day." Many of us can remember a time when comic books were considered less-than-desirable reading for children.   In 1954, the US Senate held hearings for the purpose of determining whether comic books contributed to juvenile delinquency.

We have come a long way. For fifty years, children's reading proficiency has declined. Today most children are passive receptacles for the addictive and degrading entertainment offered by video games and television. They would be better off nurturing their imagination and building their vocabularies by reading comic books. Unfortunately, the gateway to reading has been closed.

There is a sad truth behind "free comic book day." The promotion is a desperate and misguided attempt to get kids to start reading comic books again. Comic book sales are now lower then they were in the 1960s, when revolving racks of comics could be found everywhere. Today, just about the only place to buy a comic book is in a specialized comic-book store. Chuck Rozanski, who owns Mile High Comics in Denver, recently wrote "for the past fifteen years the comics business has been in an accelerating downward spiral to oblivion."

What happened? It's really quite simple. Few kids want to read modern comic books because the quality of the books is so poor. Most modern comic books are not even written for children. The art is execrable, the colors are garish, and the plots and dialogue are full of adult themes.

The comics that I used to buy for twelve cents are now two or three dollars each. They don't even look like comics. Trying to read one is an unpleasant and tense experience. The innocence, charm, and fun that constitute the heart of the comic book is missing. My eight-year-old son put it succinctly, "I like the old comics a lot better." One of the comics given away as part of "free comic book day" was a reprint of a 1947 Donald Duck story by Carl Barks. It was the best book of the lot, by far. In what other business is the quality of the product now lower than it was in 1947?

The tobacco industry, which manufactures a product for adults, has been accused of targeting children. The comic book publishers--who produce a product for children--are now targeting adults. Is it any surprise their product doesn't sell? How much longer can they continue to publish books that no child reads? Where will the next generation of readers and collectors come from?

38 CHURCHILL DISMISSAL A TRAVESTY

In July 2007, Ward Churchill was fired from his position as a tenured professor at the University of Colorado. The pretext given for his dismissal was academic misconduct. But the real reason was that professor Churchill wrote some things that offended people. His termination was a violation of the academic freedom guaranteed to faculty by the University of Colorado and the US Constitution.

We embrace free speech for pragmatic reasons. Without criticism, human knowledge cannot increase. Francis Bacon explained, "knowledge is like water, it will not rise above the level from which it fell." Intellectual freedom is essential to the progress of the human race. William Godwin understood this when he wrote that no government "should set up a standard upon the various topics of human speculation, to restrain the excursions of an inventive mind. It is only by giving a free scope to these excursions, that science, philosophy and morals have arrived at their present degree of perfection."

It is seldom the case that any of us are wise enough to discern that we are absolutely correct, or that another person is completely wrong. We should keep in mind that we are all members of a species infamous for intolerance, ignorance, and cruelty. The human race has a track record of murdering its greatest benefactors simply because they said things that offended people.

The investigation into Professor Churchill's alleged academic misconduct was a disingenuous and utterly transparent excuse for punishing him. I doubt if many faculty at the University of Colorado could withstand having their entire body of work scrutinized by a Star Chamber with a magnifying lens. Suppose I publicly criticize the local police department, and their officers subsequently start following me all over town, ticketing me for minor violations that they would normally ignore. Am I being punished for breaking the law, or for exercising my right of free speech?

I have never met Professor Churchill, and it is likely that we would disagree on many things. I approach issues from the opposite end of the political spectrum. I'm an outspoken conservative, member of the National Rifle Association, and advocate of pure nineteenth-century laissez faire capitalism. But I'm not afraid to hear viewpoints that I disagree with, and I don't seek to punish people who think differently. I listen to them, because I might learn something. Truth can only be found when there is a vigorous dialectic.

I am curious as to how the University of Colorado will carry out its mission of research and teaching, now that its faculty work in a culture of fear. A scholar cannot think and write freely if they know that they might be fired because someone is offended by their work.

In the Academy, we are supposed to inculcate intellectual diversity, not expel those we disagree with. It was Professor Churchill's duty to be controversial and offensive. He should not have been fired for doing his job. The administration of the University of Colorado has made an execrable error, one that stamps the institution with the indelible brands of ignorance and intolerance.

39 WHY THE PALEOLITHIC DIET IS NOT OPTIMAL

The Paleolithic Diet consists of foods consumed by humans during the Paleolithic period, from about 2.6 Ma to 10,000 years before present. The diet includes lean game meats, fish, eggs, vegetables, nuts, seeds, and fruits. Dairy products and grains are excluded from the Paleolithic diet.

Compared to what most Americans eat, the Paleolithic Diet is a good choice. The vast majority of Americans consume junk foods, fast foods, and processed foods in large quantities. As of 2011, two-thirds of adult Americans are overweight and one-third are obese. Obesity is correlated with an increased risk of coronary heart disease, cancer, diabetes, hypertension, stroke, and other diseases. The United States is a nation of gluttons, hurtling like a freight train toward a collision with catastrophic health costs.

If you're on the Paleolithic Diet the chances are your diet is better than that of 99 percent of the general population. But the task in designing an optimal diet is not to define what is acceptable or good, but what is best. This is an interesting area of active research that will benefit from critical discussion and analysis. In the interest of advancing human knowledge, all claims should be laid open to skeptical inspection and debate.

The theory underlying the Paleolithic Diet is that human bodies are evolutionarily adapted to living on the foods that were available to us during the two million years that *Homo erectus* evolved into *Homo sapiens*. But nature and evolution promote the survival of species, not individuals. From an evolutionary viewpoint, the optimum diet is that which guarantees the maximum number of offspring, not individual health and longevity. The health of the individual is correlated with the survival of the species, but these are not identical.

The fact that a food source was not consumed by our ancestors does not preclude the possibility that a new food source might be beneficial or even superior. Before the discovery of the Americas by Christopher Columbus, people living in Asia and Europe did not have access to chocolate. There is significant scientific evidence that regular consumption of dark chocolate inhibits the development of heart disease. Cavemen did not drink tea. But is there anyone who thinks that consumption of tea is not beneficial?

I agree that modern people probably consume too many refined grains and processed carbohydrates. But I'm not sure I understand the rationale for totally excluding grains from the Paleolithic Diet. Grains are the seeds of grasses. Why are other seeds allowed, but grass seeds excluded? And there is archeological evidence that wild grains in fact were consumed by humans living in the Paleolithic. If wild grains were not a part of our ancestor's diet, it would be very difficult to explain why they chose to cultivate these plants.

The primary drawback to the Paleolithic Diet is that it does not include dairy products. Dairy products have two significant benefits. They are high in both calcium and protein, two of the most important and hardest-to-obtain nutrients. Dairy products are also important sources of probiotics.

Protein is one of three major macronutrients utilized by the human body and is a source of amino acids used by the body for cellular growth and maintenance. The Recommended Daily Intake (RDI) of protein for an adult human is 50 g. Calcium is the most abundant mineral in the human body. The RDI for calcium is 1,000 mg. Compared to many other minerals, this is relatively high. The RDI for iron is 18 mg; for zinc, 15 mg.

There are many protein sources available to people living in affluent societies. Meats, eggs, and fish are obvious sources. But if you do not eat dairy products, it is difficult to obtain sufficient calcium in your diet without supplementation. Green leafy vegetables contain calcium. But a cup of raw Kale contains only 90 mg of calcium. I don't know anyone who eats ten cups of Kale a day. In comparison, eight ounces of plain lowfat yogurt provides 12 g of protein and 400 mg of calcium with only 130 calories. Three ounces of mozzarella cheese provide 440 mg of calcium, 19 g of protein, and 240 calories. Combine the yogurt and the cheese and you have 62 percent of your daily requirement of protein, 84 percent of the necessary calcium, but only 25 percent of a 1500-calorie energy allowance.

The cow is a miracle of nature. He takes grass, which humans cannot digest, and turns it into some of our richest and best food sources. Ruminants accomplish this remarkable feat by living in symbiosis with bacteria. The very fact that nature has designed milk as the optimal food for mammalian young should inform us that this is a food source that deserves serious consideration.

I do not endorse dairy products without caveats and qualifications. Most adults are lactose intolerant. I don't drink milk. My consumption of dairy products is confined to fermented milk products such as cheese, yogurt, and kefir. Compared to milk, these have reduced lactose and are more digestible.

If digestion is still a problem, inexpensive and convenient enzyme supplements are sold over-the-counter in health food stores.

Neither do I consume whole milk. Whole cow's milk consists of four percent fat. While a young, rapidly growing cow may need the extra calories provided by the high fat content of whole milk, it is unlikely that adult humans have the same need. So I confine my dairy consumption to lowfat cheeses and fermented milk products containing one percent fat or less.

A second reason for the inclusion of dairy products in a diet is that fermented milk products like yogurt and kefir are traditional sources of probiotics. Probiotics are an important component of the human diet. More than a hundred years ago, Elie Metchnikoff (1845-1916) theorized that consumption of soured milk would prolong human life and health.

It has subsequently been corroborated through scientific study that consumption of yogurt enhances the human immune system. In 2010, researchers reported that there are ten times more bacterial cells in the human body than human cells. "The majority of microbes reside in the gut, have a profound influence on human physiology and nutrition, and are crucial for human life." We live in symbiosis with these bacteria, and establishing and maintaining intestinal flora is essential for good health. It may be the case that animals are little more than machines constructed by bacteria to assist them in finding food.

It is possible to purchase a variety of probiotic products in the form of pills. But with yogurt or kefir you simultaneously obtain three important nutrients: protein, calcium, and probiotics. Obtaining probiotics from fermented milk products is also a more conservative choice. Foods such as yogurt have a history of traditional use that extends back for thousands of years.

The Paleolithic Diet may be natural, but "natural" is not necessarily synonymous with "good." Death and disease are natural. Most of us want a diet that promotes optimal health and longevity. In order to be useful, a philosophy must be an individual and active intellectual process rather that something that one chooses from a book. Similarly, a diet must be tailored to an individual. It must be eclectic rather than dogmatic. Designing an optimal diet requires research and a lengthy process of trial and error. Because scientific knowledge is always provisional and incomplete, it must be supplemented by an awareness of traditional use. Even anecdotal information can be useful if used properly. Every person has a biochemical uniqueness. The body has a nuanced wisdom, and there is no escape from the ultimate requirement of balancing body, mind and spirit.

I am not a physician, and none of the preceding should be taken as specific advice by any individual. I write to offer my opinion and explain the reasons for the choices I have made in my own diet.

40 SCIENCE, CONSCIENCE AND INTELLIGENT DESIGN

In 2007, Iowa State University denied tenure to astronomer Guillermo Gonzalez because of his personal belief in Intelligent Design, the philosophical proposition that the presence of order in nature is evidence for the existence of God. No one has alleged that Gonzalez taught Design or Creationism in the classroom. The issue is one of conscience.

It appears that the faculty at Iowa State do not want someone with Gonzalez's personal convictions to conduct or teach science at their institution. No administrator at Iowa State seems concerned that such discrimination is explicitly forbidden by the University's own written policy. And the fact that Gonzalez is a rising academic superstar who has published an extraordinary 68 papers in the peer-reviewed scientific literature does not appear to have helped his case. So much for the transparent lie that tenure decisions at Iowa State are based on professional merit.

But there is more to the Gonzalez case than just the latest example of intolerance at an American University. It is profoundly ironic to deny tenure to a professor who endorses Intelligent Design, because modern science was founded by men who enthusiastically embraced the Design Argument.

Although the roots of science and philosophy lie in ancient Greece, the practice of science as we know it today was first manifested by members of the Royal Society in seventeenth century England. Most of these men viewed scientific research as entirely compatible with revealed religion. In *The Christian Virtuoso* (1690), Robert Boyle stated "to embrace Christianity, I do not think I need to recede from the value and kindness I have for experimental philosophy."

The milestone that marked the beginning of the scientific era was the publication of Isaac Newton's *Principia Mathematica* in 1687. The *Principia* essentially defined how science would be conducted for the next several hundred years; it is recognized today as the greatest achievement in the history of science. The author of the *Principia*, Isaac Newton, had an extraordinary intellect. As a youth in his early twenties, he invented calculus, formulated the theory of universal gravitation, and discovered the true nature and composition of light.

In addition to being a scientist and mathematician, Isaac Newton was also a Christian fundamentalist who believed in the inerrancy of the Bible and a young Earth. He viewed the presence of mathematical order in the universe as evidence for the existence of God. After mathematically demonstrating that the movements of the planets were explained by gravitation, Newton concluded "this most beautiful system of the Sun, planets and comets, could only proceed from the counsel and dominion of an intelligent and powerful being."

For Newton, there was more than perfect consonance between science and religion. Religious faith *produced* science because it was Newton's desire to know God that motivated his study of nature and the conviction of governance by natural law. In a letter that followed the publication of the *Principia*, Newton explained "when I wrote my treatise about our system I had an eye upon such principles as might work with considering men for the belief of a Deity." In his later treatise, *Opticks* (1718), Newton explicitly argued for Intelligent Design by raising the questions, "was the eye contrived without skill in optics, and the ear without knowledge of sounds?"

Newton was not the only great scientist who believed in intelligent design, nor is the belief a relic of a lost age. In the twentieth century, Einstein said that "natural law reveals an intelligence." Thus a personal belief in Intelligent Design is not incompatible with the conduct or practice of science. Reverence for the beauty and mystery of nature is the heart of science. In Einstein's words, "science without religion is lame." In denying Professor Gonzalez his freedom of conscience, the faculty and administration at Iowa State University have demonstrated not only a cold bigotry, but an ignorance of both science and history.

41 DEIFYING DARWIN

2009 marks the 150th anniversary of the publication of Charles Darwin's groundbreaking book, *Origin of Species*. To commemorate the anniversary, the Darwin Project at the University of Oklahoma will be conducting a series of lectures, meetings, and symposia.

The anniversary of *Origin of Species* offers an opportunity to educate both students and the public, not just about evolution, but also about science as a process of discovery. Unfortunately, that is not what will happen. The Darwin Project at OU has prepared an incestuous propaganda festival. None of the invited speakers or events promises to be in any way critical of Darwin's idea. What should be an educational and scientific event will instead be a celebration of materialism and atheism. It is a breathtaking betrayal of the University's ideals of diversity and inclusiveness.

Scientific knowledge is always provisional and subject to constant revision. In order to make progress, scientists are supposed to concentrate on anomalies, areas in which the facts don't fit our theories. But all of this is thrown out the door when it comes to Darwin and evolution. The National Academy of Science has absurdly claimed that the "theory" of evolution is now a "fact," and therefore cannot be questioned.

In point of fact, Darwin's model of evolution by natural selection has never been consistent with the data. The theory predicts uniform, gradual, and continual change. Accordingly, the fossil record should contain innumerable transitional forms. It doesn't. The fossil record shows stasis punctuated by rapid change, with organisms suddenly appearing and disappearing. This was demonstrated by the French paleontologist Georges Cuvier as early as 1812, and remains true today.

Confronted with the fact that the fossil record did not support his theory, Darwin admitted that the absence of transitional forms was a grave difficulty. But rather than modify the theory to account for the facts, he instead tried to explain the evidence away. Darwin devoted an entire chapter of *Origin of Species* to what he called the "imperfection of the geological record," as if his theory were perfect and the data were defective. It is true that the geologic record is fragmentary, but nevertheless the extant sections do not support Darwin's theory. The gradual change predicted by Darwin is simply not present.

Darwin's theory was badly flawed, but it was celebrated because it enabled science to explain everything and dominate the entire world of knowledge. Prior to *Origin of Species*, science had no way of explaining the origin of living things. Christian theology was evicted from science, but materialism and atheism crept in the back door. Unlike other scientific theories, Darwinism cannot be replaced, or even criticized, because it provides the foundation for metaphysical and religious concepts.

I am not a creationist, and am as skeptical of traditional religion as Hume or Voltaire. But the doctrines of materialism and atheism have no more foundation than revealed religion, and probably less. It is impossible to be sure that God does not exist. The most brilliant and original thinkers who ever lived, the Greek philosophers, embraced monotheism long before the Christian era. To assert, as a materialist does, that nothing exists outside of the material world revealed to us by our senses, is equivalent to the oxymoronic claim that one knows the unknown. It is the doctrine of a person that is incapable of critical insight or intellectual reflection.

Naturalism is essential to science, but I'm not sure if it is a good idea for science to lay claim to the entire world of knowledge. Science does not tell us how to order our civilizations. It cannot define morality. If the atheists are right, and God does not exist, then the concepts of good and evil are meaningless. All we are left with is Darwin's struggle for existence, where might makes right and the end justifies the mean.

Science should be a disinterested search for knowledge based on observation and reason, free from any ideological or religious constraint. But instead of freedom from religion, we have simply substituted one faith for another. Christianity has been replaced by the doctrines of materialism and atheism. The zealous followers of these doctrines masquerade as scholars and scientists, but relentlessly seek to stifle all criticism, dissent, and inquiry. They are the enemies of both religion and science.

42 DOUBTING DARWIN

Some time ago I received an email asking how, as a scientist and geologist, I could associate myself with the Discovery Institute by signing their Dissent from Darwinism statement. The statement reads, in toto, "We are skeptical of claims for the ability of random mutation and natural selection to account for the complexity of life. Careful examination of the evidence for Darwinian theory should be encouraged."

My critic seemed to think that anyone who would agree with this statement was necessarily a creationist, if not a Biblical fundamentalist that believed the Earth was 6,000 years old. On the contrary, I'm an evolutionist. I'm committed to naturalism in science, and I believe that radioactive dating and other evidence shows the Earth to be about 4.6 billion years old.

The reason I'm an evolutionist is that science is based largely on empirical evidence. The fossil record shows progressive change in life through time. The farther back we go in time, the more that life diverges from present day forms. If we do nothing but look at the fossils, we see a process of natural change, or evolution.

There is no scientific reason that one-hundred percent of biologists and geologists should not sign the *Dissent from Darwinism* statement. Who can disagree that "careful examination of the evidence" is indicated for every scientific theory? And there is plenty of skepticism in the scientific literature regarding the ability of natural selection alone to account for the changes we infer from the fossil record. A 2009 paper published in the *Proceedings of the National Academy of Science* began with the words "I reject the Darwinian assumption...[of] a single common ancestor." A 2005 review paper published in *Trends in Ecology and Evolution* noted that "the many intermediate forms hypothesized by Darwin" were "missing." These are but two examples that illustrate a pervasive theme of skeptical deliberation.

With the possible exception of global warming, I am not aware of any other area in science where scientists can be so unscientific, close-minded, and dogmatic. Darwin is a sacred cow that cannot be questioned. Especially in the field of zoology, there is a fanatical core of atheists and materialists who have created a false dichotomy. One must either accept Darwinian evolution as dogma or risk being labeled as a Biblical fundamentalist. But in fact there are alternative theories of evolution that do not rely primarily upon natural selection.

The single largest problem with Darwin's theory of evolution by natural selection is that it contradicts the fossil record. The theory predicts uniform, gradual, and continual change. If Darwin's theory were correct, *every* fossil would be a transitional form. But transitional fossils are rare. As early as 1812, Georges Cuvier (1769-1832) documented that the fossil record shows stasis punctuated by rapid change. Organisms suddenly appear and disappear. Transitional fossils are not unknown, but they are scarce. A 2009 paper published in the *Proceedings of the Royal Society* noted "the relative rarity of truly informative fossil intermediates."

If one should happen to mention that transitional fossils are uncommon, Darwinists typically respond that is it not true that there are no transitional fossils. But no one ever said that transitional fossils don't exist, only that they are rare. Distorting an opponent's position into a distorted straw-man that is easily knocked down is a classic intellectual fallacy. Debating a dogmatic Darwinist can be frustrating, because it's like arguing with a twelve-year-old child that has no critical thinking skills.

If Darwinists are oblivious to the empirical data, they're only acting in the best tradition. It was Darwin himself who initiated the practice of explaining away the evidence. But in fact the story begins much earlier.

In the sixth century BC what we know today as science began when the Greek natural philosophers rejected supernatural explanations and invoked naturalism. The necessary corollary to naturalism is uniformity, the supposition that nature acts uniformly and predictably throughout both space and time. Without uniformity, naturalist explanations are no better than supernatural. Unless nature acts according to uniform and invariant law, its acts are as capricious as those of the gods. With naturalism and uniformity, the universe became a cosmos, an ordered place that could be understood through observation and reason.

In *Principia Mathematica* (1687) Isaac Newton characterized uniformity as the "foundation of all philosophy." Newton was not only the greatest physicist of all time, he was also a Biblical fundamentalist who believed that the Earth was no more than a few thousand years old. Newton advocated intelligent design, and wrote that "the true God is a living, intelligent, and powerful Being," not an abstract spiritual principle. But ironically, Newton was also the godfather of Charles Darwin.

The line of academic descent from Newton to Darwin is unmistakable. The Scottish mathematician, Colin Maclaurin (1698-1746), was a protege of Isaac Newton. At the University of Edinburgh, one of Maclaurin's students was the geologist, James Hutton (1726-1797). In the English and American tradition, Hutton is recognized as the founder of the modern science of geology because he was the first to insist on uniformity.

But James Hutton had little contemporary influence because his writing was terribly prolix. The person who really founded uniformitarian geology was Charles Lyell (1797-1875). Lyell wrote *Principles of Geology* as an exposition of Hutton's uniformitarian geology. The book was published in twelve editions from 1830 through 1875. Enormously influential, Lyell's *Principles* virtually created the modern science of geology. Among Lyell's readers was the young Charles Darwin. Darwin took a copy with him on the voyage of the Beagle, and later wrote "I studied [*Principles*] attentively; and the book was of the highest service to me in many ways."

Lyell was the single largest influence on Darwin. Darwin dedicated his book, *Voyage of the Beagle* (1839), to Lyell. In his autobiography, Darwin confessed "I saw more of Lyell than any other man." After Darwin published *Origin of Species* (1859) he was warmly congratulated by Lyell.

But Charles Lyell was largely a polemicist and scientific fraud. It was Lyell who taught Darwin to ignore evidence that contradicted theory. Lyell's *Principles* was not so much a textbook on geology as a polemical argument for an extreme form of uniformity. Lyell went far beyond Newton and the ancient Greeks. He espoused a radical uniformitarianism that relied not just upon invariant natural law, but invoked, without justification, uniform causes, processes, and rates over geologic time. These were Lyell's "principles" of geology.

In a letter written shortly before the first edition of *Principles* was published, Lyell admitted that "all my geology will come in as illustration of my views of those principles." In other words, Lyell frankly admitted his intention to reverse the normal scientific process. Instead of collecting facts and inductively inferring a plausible and testable theory, Lyell intended to start with a theory and then selectively search for facts that supported his preconceived idea.

Lyell worked overtime at torturing the evidence to fit into his theoretical framework. If the geological facts appeared to contradict absolute uniformity, Lyell's favorite trick was to dismiss the evidence as inconclusive.

In the nineteenth century geologists found fossilized ferns on the frigid island of Spitzbergen, north of Iceland. If tropical plants once grew north of the Arctic Circle, it was evidence of dramatic or even catastrophic climate change. But such change was antithetical to Lyell's rigid uniformitarianism. Confronted with apparently irrefutable evidence of climate change, Lyell confessed "I have tried in all my travels to persuade myself that the evidence was inconclusive."

Darwin's theory of evolution by natural selection is nothing but the uniformitarian geology of Hutton and Lyell applied to biology. No one questions natural selection. The fact that those organisms who are best adapted to their environment are the ones that survive and reproduce is a virtual tautology. But that doesn't answer the critical question. Does natural selection have the creative power to account for the dramatic changes we see in the fossil record?

Darwin himself was aware of the problem. He characterized the lack of intermediate forms in the fossil record as "the most obvious and serious objection which can be urged against the theory." Following Lyell's example, Darwin argued that if the geologic evidence failed to match his theory, it was because the fossil record was too fragmentary to be conclusive. He devoted an entire chapter of *Origin of Species* to what he termed the "imperfection of the geological record."

The fossil or geological record is indeed incomplete. In the year 1859, Darwin's argument was plausible. But more than a hundred and fifty years of fossil collecting has not produced the missing fossils or corroborated Darwin's theory. Transitional fossils remain rare. Life on Earth for the last several hundred million years has been characterized by stasis punctuated by episodic and rapid change.

None of this is an argument for supernaturalism. There are many *scientific* alternatives to natural selection. Endosymbiotic theory proposes that multi-celled organisms arose not through natural selection, but through the interaction of single-celled bacteria. We beginning to become aware that horizontal gene transfer may have played an important role in evolution. We don't know how life began, and we don't understand all the mechanisms by which life evolved on Earth. And we most certainly are not aware of what we don't know. It is relatively easy for us to assess the extent of our knowledge, but impossible to fathom the extent of our ignorance.

Instead of dogmatically insisting that we have all the answers, we ought to be highlighting gaps in our knowledge. And there are many. Thomas Kuhn wrote that discovery in science "commences with the awareness of anomaly." By "anomaly," Kuhn meant an area where facts do not match theory. We can't make positive progress unless we first focus on the negative. This is the lesson that Socrates taught in the fifth century BC.

In 2008, I published a critique of intelligent design theory in the peer-reviewed journal *Earth Science Reviews*. I concluded that intelligent design cannot be construed as a scientific theory, and that the apparent goal of the intelligent design movement was to restore Christian theology as the queen of the sciences.

But I also argued that to the extent creationists were highlighting areas in which scientific theory was inadequate they were doing better science than biologists. We ought to stop pretending that science has all the answers. Science is an empirical system of knowledge, and we never have all the data. It is the fate of every scientific theory to be superseded. Even the invincible edifice of Newtonian mechanics crumbled before the onslaught of relativity theory.

And that's why I signed the Discovery Institute's *Dissent from Darwinism*. Not because I'm a creationist, but because I'm a scientist. Religion is conservative and dogmatic. But science is progressive and skeptical. We can't save science by turning it into religion.

43 COMPARING CHRISTIANITY AND ISLAM

Christianity and Islam are the largest religions in the world. Thirty-three percent of the world's population are Christian, twenty-one percent Muslim. The world's two largest religions have much in common, but are also different in some crucial ways. The origins of both religions are fully described in my book, *Science and Technology in World History, Volume 2*.

Both Christianity and Islam are offshoots of Judaism. From Judaism, Christianity and Islam derived the doctrines of monotheism, prophecy, resurrection, and a belief in the existence of heaven and hell.

Both Islam and Christianity have a holy book. Christians consider the Bible to be the inspired word of God. But Muslims believe that the Koran is the literal word of God. Mohammed was merely transcribing the words of Allah much as a court reporter does. Muslims therefore attribute greater spiritual authenticity to the Koran and Islam than to the Bible and Christianity.

In Catholicism, salvation is obtained through the sacraments of the Church, including baptism, penance, and the Eucharist. Most Protestant denominations hold the doctrine that salvation depends solely on faith in Jesus Christ. But in Islam, salvation is through works and is not limited to Muslims.

Christianity is focused on forgiveness, charity, and mercy, with a side dressing of apocalyptic visions, Hell, and the wrath of God. But Islam is centered on justice and the destruction of unbelievers. Allah is merciful—but not to infidels. The early history of Christianity is one of persecution and martyrdom. Jesus himself submitted to crucifixion. In contrast, Islam was not born in submission and earnest entreaty, but in warfare against the enemies of God.

After the *Hegira*, Mohammed and his followers began a jihad against their pagan enemies in Mecca. At the Battle of Badr in 624 AD, Mohammed's servant found one of his master's enemies lying wounded on the battlefield. He cut off the man's head and presented to Mohammed as a present. The Prophet was overjoyed. He exclaimed, "the head of the enemy of God! It is more acceptable to me than the choicest camel in all Arabia." After the bodies of his foes were cast into a pit, Mohammed stood at the edge of the pit and taunted the dead by asking "have you found that what God threatened is true?"

Consider how Jesus and Mohammed handled what was essentially the same problem. A woman who had committed adultery was brought before Jesus for judgment. As she had been caught in the very act, there was no question of her guilt. The sentence dictated by Mosaic Law was death by stoning but Jesus showed mercy. He said, "he that is without sin among you, let him first cast a stone at her." Embarrassed, the woman's accusers dropped their rocks and walked away. Jesus told the woman to go home and repent. But when a man and a woman who had committed adultery (with each other) were brought before Mohammed, he exclaimed "stone them," and the pair was executed.

Christians tend to attribute greater spiritual authenticity to Christianity because of its emphasis on mercy and forgiveness. But in fact the God of the Christians is as unrelenting as Allah in His condemnation of unbelievers. In *Luke*, Jesus described how God tortured a rich man in Hell by burning him. In the parable of the wheat and the tares, Jesus proclaimed that at the Last Judgment God would send out angels to gather the "children of the wicked one" and "cast them into a furnace of fire."

No faith has an unblemished history of extending charity to the enemies of God. When Christian Crusaders captured Jerusalem in 1099 AD they massacred the Muslims and Jews. Raymond of Aguilers claimed that "men rode in blood up to their knees and bridle reins." This was no doubt an exaggeration, but nevertheless an indication of terrible mayhem. To the atrocities committed under the banner of Christianity we could add the Inquisition, the Witch Mania, and the infamous *Malleus Maleficarum* (*Hammer of the Witches*), first published in 1487 AD.

The roots of Christian charity lay in the ethics advocated by the Hebrew prophets. But the Jews also killed the enemies of God. In the book of *Deuteronomy*, God gave the Hebrews license to destroy their enemies and plunder their cities. "Thou shalt smite them, and utterly destroy them; thou shalt make no covenant with them, nor show mercy unto them."

We know more about Mohammed than Jesus, because he was recognized during his lifetime as the founder of Islam. Thus there were contemporary biographies and written records. In contrast, no one recognized Jesus as an important person in his own lifetime. Even as late as fifty years after his death, Jesus remained nearly a complete unknown to the Mediterranean world. Our primary sources for the life and teachings of Jesus are the Gospels. And the Gospels were never intended to be objective historical documents. They were written to proselytize. The author of *John* explained that "these are written so that you may believe."

Women have an inferior status in both Christianity and Islam. God first created Adam (*Genesis* 2). Eve was sort of an afterthought, manufactured purely to be a helper and companion for the man, Adam. And it was the scheming Eve who created original sin by talking the guileless Adam into eating the forbidden fruit. The Apostle Paul forbade women to speak in church and instructed them to submit to their husbands. According to Paul, the man was not "created for the woman, but the woman for the man."

In Sura 4.34, the Koran plainly states that men are superior to women. Women are instructed to dress modestly. A virtuous woman is one who is obedient. If she is not obedient, her husband is allowed to scourge her. But the husband is admonished to refrain from punishing a virtuous woman.

In the West, religion is largely treated as a matter of conscience and there is a tradition of freedom of religion. But Islam is a way of life, not just a personal belief. Individual behavior is specified in the Koran. Gambling and the consumption of both pork and alcohol are forbidden. Slavery is allowed, but slave owners are admonished to treat their servants well. Fornication is punishable by scourging. To allow individual transgressions would undermine the moral fabric that binds Islamic societies together.

Perhaps no aspect of Islam is more misunderstood by Western Christians than its role in government. Jesus began a tradition of divorcing Christianity from secular government by declaring that people should not confuse secular and spiritual obligations. "Render therefore unto Caesar the things which are Caesar's; and unto God the things that are God's." Jesus also said, "my kingdom is not of this world."

But there is no tradition of separating government and religion in Islam. Indeed, such a separation would likely strike a Muslim as insane. Government exists to enforce moral rules of behavior, and morality is defined by religion. The two are therefore inexorably intertwined. This was also understood to be the case in Christian Europe before the Reformation and even well after. Freedom of religion in Protestant Germany was not individual religious freedom, but the freedom for each ruling prince to determine the orthodoxy in his polity.

Government in Islamic countries is necessarily theocratic. The Koran is a handbook for an entire system of government. In *Life of Mahomet*, William Muir explained, "Scattered throughout...[the Koran are]...the archives of a theocratic government in all its departments...The elements of a code both criminal and civil are...introduced. Punishments for certain offences are specified, and a mass of legislation laid down for the tutelage of orphans, for marriage, divorce, sales, bargains, wills, evidence, usury and similar concerns."

Westerners seem oblivious to the fact that not everyone in the world believes in the superiority of democratic government. The Greek system of democracy is foreign to Islam. Muslims no more appreciate having a democratic government forced upon them than westerners would like being forced to live under an Islamic theocracy.

God does not speak to me, so I cannot make any substantive comment on the degree to which any religion may be correct or incorrect. However, no matter what our personal beliefs are, it is important that we recognize the significant differences between Christianity and Islam.

44 MODEST PROPOSALS

As of the fall of 2008, it is apparent that our country is tied in a knot. Bogged down in two foreign wars, we now find ourselves with an economic crisis at home. I have some modest proposals that I believe will solve many of our problems.

Like many people, I'm baffled at the reluctance of the Iraqis to embrace the democratic system we are seeking to impose on them. Admittedly, a western-style liberal democracy is entirely foreign to their culture and religion. But this is no reason to reject our assistance, especially when we accompany our blessings with high explosives. What can you do with unreasonable people? History provides the answer.

The person who really knew how to deal with the Middle East was Alexander the Great. Alexander had the funny idea that when you make war, you should defeat your enemy, not yourself. He also expected to turn a profit, and would accept nothing less than complete victory. When the cities of Tyre and Gaza declined to be conquered, Alexander besieged them, killed all who resisted, and sold the survivors into slavery. Selling defeated enemies to the slave merchant was not only profitable, but a humane alternative to their execution.

Since the Iraqis are being obstinate, I suggest we sell the entire population of twenty-eight million--men, women, and children--into slavery. Once Iraq has been emptied of its troublesome native population, we can lease it to Exxon-Mobile with the understanding that they are to provide the US with oil in return for a fair profit. Energy crisis solved!

A minor impediment to this plan is the regrettable fact there is currently no market for slaves because no nation in the world today officially permits slavery. However, I believe many third-world countries could be intimidated into changing their policies by threat of nuclear bombardment. The proper way to begin would probably be to make an example of an especially obnoxious regime. I suggest detonating a small atomic bomb on the site of the presidential palace in Zimbabwe. This would have the desirable side effect of rewarding us with the undying gratitude of the Zimbabwean people.

Some people might express horror at the prospect of using atomic weapons. But a little nuclear chastisement never hurt anyone. Look at what it did for Japan. The angry militaristic nation that bombed Pearl Harbor was turned into a productive and peaceful country that supplies us with marvelous cameras.

When Iraqi oil has been utterly depleted, the real estate could be sold to Israel. The sale of slaves, oil, and land would thus turn an unprofitable and ill-advised venture into a lucrative and happy enterprise.

Other opportunities suggest themselves. When Ronald Reagan invaded Grenada in 1983, the war was won handily in fifteen minutes. The hostile Grenadians were successfully subdued and have not bothered us since. By picking a war he could win, Reagan proved himself smarter than George Bush. But I think we could do better still by invading a country that was not only pathetically weak, but rich.

Conquering Canada would be a piece of cake. Technically, they have a military, but realistically the only opposition will come from the Mounted Police. There will be no problem with the population, because the Canadians have disarmed themselves with gun-control policies. Certainly, the element of surprise would be on our side. By the time the Canadians woke to the tanks in their streets, it would be all over. The invasion could be morally justified by the fact that in some places in Canada there are people who (gasp) speak French.

Having quickly subdued Canada, we could then turn it into a satrapy, letting the Canadians do whatsoever they pleased, so long as they paid us a stiff tax. The income from Canada could be used to provide all US citizens with free medical services. Health care crisis solved!

I'm aware that my modest proposals may rouse the indignation of the world, especially that of our friends, the Europeans. But in fact I am only proposing that we fulfill the expectations of our continental colleagues, as they already consider Americans to be both barbarous and ignorant. Europeans, in contrast, are the most moral and enlightened people on earth. It is true that in past centuries they burned people alive for having the wrong religion, or for the dastardly crime of thinking the wrong thoughts. But our dear friends have made considerable progress. In the last century, they set the standard by blessing humanity with World War I, World War II, and the Holocaust. Can we do any less?

45 HOW EUROPEANS INVENTED THE MODERN WORLD

Both Greece and Rome made significant contributions to Western Civilization. Greek knowledge was ascendant in philosophy, physics, chemistry, medicine, and mathematics for nearly two thousand years.

The Romans did not have the Greek temperament for philosophy and science, but they had a genius for law and civil administration. The Romans were also great engineers and builders. They invented concrete, perfected the arch, and constructed roads and bridges that remain in use today.

But neither the Greeks nor the Romans had much appreciation for technology. As documented in my book, *Science and Technology in World History, Volume 2*, the technological society that transformed the world was conceived by Europeans during the Middle Ages.

Greeks and Romans were notorious in their disdain for technology. Aristotle noted that to be engaged in the mechanical arts was "illiberal and irksome." Seneca infamously characterized invention as something fit only for "the meanest slaves." The Roman Emperor Vespasian rejected technological innovation for fear it would lead to unemployment.

Greek and Roman economies were built on slavery. Strabo described the slave market at Delos as capable of handling the sale of 10,000 slaves a day. With an abundant supply of manual labor, the Romans had little incentive to develop artificial or mechanical power sources. Technical occupations such as blacksmithing came to be associated with the lower classes.

With the collapse of the Western Roman Empire in the fifth century AD, a Dark Age in philosophy and science descended upon the Mediterranean region. But the unwritten history of technological progress continued. In northern and western Europe, there was never a period of regression. As early as 370 AD, an unknown author noted the "mechanical inventiveness" of the "barbarian peoples" of northern Europe.

The Christian ethic of universal brotherhood slowly spread through Europe and slavery began to disappear. Tribes and peoples became united under a common creed. Europeans not only embraced technology, they also developed the idea of a universal society based upon respect for the dignity and worth of the individual human being.

From the sixth through the ninth centuries AD, Europeans adopted new agricultural technologies that dramatically increased productivity. One of these innovations was a heavy wheeled plow that broke up the soil more efficiently than the Roman "scratch" plow. Formerly unproductive lands were transformed into arable cropland.

The Greeks and Romans had harnessed horses with a throat-and-girth harness that consisted of a strap placed across the animal's neck. As soon as the horse began to pull, he would choke himself. In the ninth century, Europeans began to use a padded horse collar that transferred the load of a draught animal to its shoulders. Horses harnessed with collars were able to pull four to five times more weight than those with throat-and-girth harnesses.

Horse power was also facilitated by the introduction of the iron shoe. With fast-moving horses harnessed efficiently, it became possible to transport goods up to 35 kilometers in one day if a sufficiently good road was available. There was now a way to dispose of agricultural surpluses and create wealth that could be used for investment in technology and infrastructure. Thus the introduction of the lowly horse shoe and collar fostered commerce, civilization, and the growth of towns.

Under the Roman system of two-field crop rotation, half the land was left fallow and unproductive at any given time. In the eighth century, Europeans began to practice three-field crop rotation. Fields lay fallow for only a third of the year, and grains were alternated with legumes that enriched the soil with nitrogen. The cultivation of legumes such as peas and beans added valuable protein to European diets.

In the tenth century, the climate began to warm and Europe entered the High Middle Ages. By the thirteenth century, the new agricultural technologies had doubled per acre yields. Population surged; architecture and commerce flourished. Europeans began a program of aggressive territorial expansion. They reclaimed Sicily in 1090 and systematically drove Muslims out of Spain. The First Crusade was launched in 1095, and Jerusalem was captured from the Seljukian Turks in 1099.

The prosperity created by the new agricultural technologies subsidized education and the growth of knowledge. In the late eighth century, Charlemagne revived education in Europe by setting up a general system of schools. For the first time, not just monks but the general public was educated. As the European economy prospered, students multiplied and traveled, seeking the best education they could find. Christian Cathedral Schools evolved into the first universities. The Universities of Paris and Oxford were founded c. 1170, Cambridge in 1209 AD.

The harnessing of water power began around 200 BC with the invention of the *quern*, a primitive grain mill consisting of two rotating stones. The Romans had been aware of water power, but made little use of water wheels and mills. In contrast, by the tenth century, Europeans had begun a wholesale conversion of their civilization from human and animal-power to water power. The water-mill came to be viewed not just as a grain mill, but as a generalized source of power that could be adopted for many uses. This new approach was to fundamentally alter the fabric of human civilization.

By the thirteenth century, water power was being utilized in sawmills, tanning mills, and iron forges. Mechanical power derived from moving water was used to process beer mash, to turn wood lathes and grinding stones, to power bellows, to drive forge hammers, and to manufacture paper.

Because water power was only available where streams were located, Europeans developed other sources of mechanical power. Tidal power was used in Dover and Venice in the eleventh century. The first windmill in Europe appeared in 1085 AD. Over the next hundred years, windmill technology spread rapidly over the plains of northern Europe. Windmills provided power in the cold of winter when water mills were shut down by frozen streams.

The utilization of mechanical power in these many forms required that Europeans develop methods for transferring and redirecting power, crucial technologies for the Industrial Revolution of the late eighteenth century. Most important of these was the crank. The *crank* is a device that allows rotary motion to converted into reciprocal motion, or vice versa. For an industrial or technological civilization, the importance of the crank is second only to that of the wheel itself. Without the crank, "machine civilization is inconceivable."

Water clocks had been known since ancient times, but were notoriously inaccurate and inconvenient. Near the end of the thirteenth century, it became possible to construct the first mechanical clock when some unknown genius invented a device known as the *verge escapement.* The verge escapement enabled the power delivered by a falling weight to be modulated and delivered evenly at a constant rate. The techniques developed in clockwork for regulating and transferring power were essential for the complex machinery of the Industrial Revolution.

The introduction of mechanical clocks also made it feasible to adopt standardized time keeping. This was a necessary step for the eventual development of a technological civilization that needs to coordinate complex administrative and commercial interactions.

Modern science traces its roots to the natural philosophy of the ancient Greeks and the presocratic enlightenment c. 600-400 BC. The Greeks began the evolution of what became modern science by introducing naturalism and rejecting supernatural explanations. Describing epilepsy, a Hippocratic author noted that the disease was "no more divine nor more sacred than other diseases, but has a natural cause from which it originates like other affections."

But neither the Greeks nor the Romans ever hit upon the experimental method. Greek philosophers favored the deductive logic used in geometry. They had several reasons for being skeptical of a science based on observation. The world was in state of continual flux, different people observed things differently, and the only data available to them were anecdotal.

Modern science began in the thirteenth century when Christian theologians such as Robert Grossesteste became seduced by Aristotelian logic and the Greek principle of demonstrative proof. But when Grosseteste and his student Roger Bacon contemplated the mysterious properties of the magnet, they were forced to conclude that logic alone could never uncover the secrets of the cosmos. Magnetism was a phenomenon that could never be predicted by logical reasoning. It could only be observed. Thus the need for a systematic experimental method.

Gunpowder originated in China, but firearms were a European invention. Cannon date from the first part of the fourteenth century in Europe, and were common by 1350. The use of cannon in particular helped break up feudalism, as it made central fortifications obsolete. Even the strongest structures were now vulnerable. The protection offered by a stone castle was eviscerated.

The possession of personal firearms gave individuals more political power, and was an engine for social and political change. The firearm was also the first internal combustion engine, and demonstrated the enormous potential power that lay in confined and controlled combustion.

Like gunpowder, many of the technologies developed and utilized by Europeans originated in China. But the Chinese were never able to fully develop the promise of these inventions because their economic development was strangled by a "bureaucratic, state controlled economy."

In Europe, the leaders in developing medieval technology were not philosophers, but craftsmen, merchants, and businessmen. In a word, entrepreneurs. There were profits to be derived from the new technologies. A water-powered mill required a considerable capital investment, but the investment was likely to return a significant profit. Inventive, free people looked for ways to improve their productivity. Individuals profited and society prospered.

Thus the Industrial Revolution that began in England c. 1760 was the inevitable outcome of a thousand years of European technological progress fostered by economic freedom. During the nineteenth and twentieth centuries, the technological innovations pioneered in Europe began to spread throughout the world. This process continues today, most notably with the transformation of the world's most populous countries, China and India.

The most undeniable benefit of the technology that Europeans bequeathed to the world was a dramatic increase in life expectancy. Before the Industrial Revolution, average life expectancy at birth was only 25 years, no higher than it had been in Roman times. But as of 2010, life expectancy in the world had reached 70 years. And Japanese women now enjoy a record life expectancy at birth of 86 years.

Thus the world was transformed, not by philosophers, scientists, or politicians, but by engineers, craftsmen, and entrepreneurs. Writing in 1768, Joseph Priestley predicted "whatever was the beginning of this world, the end will be glorious and paradisaical, beyond what our imaginations can now conceive." Thanks to European inventors, Priestley's prediction was fulfilled.

46 ANIMADVERSIONS ON ATHEISM

Atheism is on the upswing. The University of Oklahoma recently announced the formation of a student club dedicated to atheism and skepticism. Of course atheists tend to be only skeptical of theism and never atheism. Living among human beings, we are constantly reminded that ignorance is the normal human condition.

The *Oxford English Dictionary* defines an atheist as "one who denies or disbelieves the existence of a God." Atheism is distinct from agnosticism. The agnostic professes no belief in God but does not deny the possibility of God's existence.

The dictionary is of less help when it comes to defining God. God may be an entity, "the Creator and Ruler of the universe," or an impersonal principle, "the supreme or ultimate reality." There are as many definitions of God as there are religions. Cicero tells us that the opinions of men on this subject are "various and different." For the purpose of this essay, I follow Anselm of Canterbury (1033-1109 AD) in defining God as a Being, a reality, or an abstract spiritual principle of "which nothing greater can be conceived." As a transcendent spiritual reality, God, by Its very definition, must be beyond human comprehension, although not entirely beyond human apprehension. I am aware, for example, of the existence of many fields of higher study in mathematics and physics that I barely comprehend. I do not have to fully understand these subjects to be aware that they exist.

I have said nothing of my own belief in this matter. I write not to profess or proselytize, but to critique and argue, to explore and learn. The person who can point out my mistakes "shall carry off the palm, not as an enemy, but as a friend." I have no need to believe--it is better to understand than to believe. I confess only an affection for Pyrrhonian skepticism, the philosophical position that nothing can be known for certain. But certainly many things may be known with degrees of probability.

There is nothing new about either monotheism or atheism. Monotheism may have been known in Egypt and Babylonia as early as 1500 BC. The first of the Greek philosophers to reject polytheism and propose a type of monotheism was reportedly Xenophanes (c. 570-475 BC). Empedocles (c. 492-432 BC) described God as "only mind, sacred and ineffable mind, flashing through the whole universe with swift thoughts." For Aristotle (384-322 BC), "the actuality of thought is life, and God is that actuality."

There are scattered reports of atheists among the ancient Greeks. As described in my book, *Science and Technology in World History, Volume 1*, methodological naturalism arose among the presocratic Ionians and Hippocratic physicians in the 5th and 6th centuries BC. Epicureans were atomists and materialists who rejected teleology in nature. Epicurus (341-270 BC) professed a belief in the gods, but his deities were abstract spiritual beings that never interacted with, or took an interest in, the affairs of human beings. It is a just inference to conclude that antiquity held many atheists who nursed their convictions in secret to avoid prosecution for impiety.

In *Lives of the Eminent Philosophers*, Diogenes Laërtius (3rd cent. AD) informs us that Theodorus (c. 340-250 BC) "utterly discarded all previous opinions about the gods." In the 5th century BC, the poet Diagoras had to flee Athens to avoid prosecution on charges of atheism. Both Diagoras and Theodorus are also mentioned by Cicero (106-43 BC) as examples of philosophers who did not believe in the gods. From the scanty evidence it is not clear if Diagoras and Theodorus were atheists in the modern sense, or merely skeptics who mocked the popular polytheistic conception of anthropomorphic gods.

Western Civilization has become increasingly more secular for the last thousand years. The process began when Christian theologians in Europe were seduced by Greek logic, and is outlined in the second volume of my history of science. Anselm of Canterbury (1033-1109 AD) sought to construct an argument for the existence of God that was based entirely on logic. Anselm's approach was cemented by Thomas Aquinas, and Scholasticism became the predominant intellectual school in Europe for the next few centuries. Both Anselm and Aquinas claimed to place faith before reason. But in using reason to justify faith, they unwittingly acquiesced to the superiority of reason.

In 1543, Copernicus' *Revolutions*, a technical work in astronomy, began the process of unraveling the unity of the medieval European world by removing the Earth from the center of the cosmos. Many of the icons of the Scientific Revolution were devout Christians and fervent theists. Johannes Kepler, Robert Boyle, and Isaac Newton all viewed experimental philosophy as entirely consistent with, and complementary to, Christianity. But the

Scientific Revolution replaced revelation by observation and reason. Consideration of final purposes was excluded from experimental philosophy. The epistemological revolution was completed during the eighteenth-century Enlightenment.

Newtonian physics explained the mechanical universe through the impersonal action of natural law. But scientists and philosophers still needed God to explain the origin of life. At the beginning of the nineteenth century, we find Richard Kirwan, the President of the Royal Irish Academy, maintaining that "geology graduates into religion." In 1829, the Royal Society of England undertook the publication of the *Bridgewater Treatises*, works that were commissioned to illustrate "the power, wisdom, and goodness of God."

In 1859 Darwin published *Origin of Species*. Darwin's theory was proposed to explain the evolution of life, but was subsequently invoked to implicitly explain the origin of life. After Darwin, God was no longer necessary to answer scientific questions. By the end of the nineteenth century God had been expelled from the sciences. On April 8, 1966, *Time Magazine* published the infamous red-and-black cover that posed the question, "Is God Dead?" The secularization of Western society was not yet complete, but certainly substantial.

The atheist views this historical process as the inevitable triumph of human progress. "Science," Carl Sagan assured us, is a "candle in the dark" that dispels the "demon-haunted world." Religion and theism are to be extinguished the same way that the diseases of polio and smallpox were conquered. God is just another superstition that must be eradicated to further the march of human progress. "Imagine," the songwriter says, a world with no religion. Then we will all live happily together in a peaceful communistic utopia.

To the atheist, religion, especially the Christian religion, is the spawning ground of horrors and atrocities. The Witch Mania and the Spanish Inquisition were perpetrated under the guise of Christianity. Before the Reformation, the Catholic Church and papacy were dens of iniquity and hypocrisy. In 1501, Pope Alexander VI presided over the infamous Banquet of the Chestnuts at which fifty naked prostitutes danced. After the Reformation, men had other men burned to death over disagreements on minor and obscure points of religious doctrine. Not only did Catholics fight with Protestants, the Protestant sects fought with each other. In 1553 John Calvin had Michael Servetus arrested and executed. Johannes Kepler was refused the sacrament of communion because he would not accept the Doctrine of Ubiquity. And there is much truth in the traditional view that religion and science are antagonistic systems of knowledge. Rational philosophy and the sciences were expelled from Islamic civilization in the twelfth century by religious fundamentalists.

I acknowledge the preceding, but because something has been at times abused or corrupted does not convince me that it should be altogether discarded. Intolerance is not so much the product of religion as it is the normal human condition. Religion, like science, can be both used and abused. Science tells us how to make both antibiotics and mustard gas. The science of chemistry informs the manufacture of explosives. Explosive chemicals can be fruitfully applied in mining and civil engineering, but they can also be used to murder. Science is inherently amoral. Perhaps we object more strenuously when religion is abused because religion has pretensions to moral authority.

The sciences complement our technologies and satisfy our intellectual curiosity. But science does not inform morality or tell us how to build and order human civilizations. Impressed by Isaac Newton's physics, John Locke expressed the hope that morality could be made into an exact science. But like much Enlightenment rhetoric, Locke's hope has proven to be chimerical. We have social sciences such as psychology, sociology, and anthropology. But these are not exact sciences. The extent to which they provide us with reliable information is constrained by inherent limitations. It is difficult to accurately define and measure psychological variables, and separating the effects of multiple compounding factors can be problematical. Controlled experiments with human beings usually cannot be conducted for ethical reasons. And the sciences can only tell us how people *do* act, not how they *should* act.

There is no science that addresses final causes or existential questions. It is religion that does these things. If atrocities have been perpetrated under the cloak of religion, it nonetheless must be admitted that religion and theism have had beneficial influences. What we call Western Civilization today is largely the result of grafting Christian charity onto Greek rationalism. Christianity provided the notion that all men are brothers. This is the ethic of a global-scale civilization. Christianity was instrumental in uniting the diverse tribes and cultures of Europe. It fostered unity, the growth of nations and commerce. Francis Bacon asserted that the progress of the sciences required mass cooperation. It therefore seems undeniable that Christianity and other religions have synergistically promoted scientific activity to the extent that they have encouraged people to get along peacefully.

We need both science and religion. Since *Homo erectus* walked the Earth, humanity has been defined by its use of technology. We are not the only animal that uses knowledge and tools to manipulate the natural environment, but we do so to such an exaggerated degree that it virtually defines us as a species. And we are a social animal that lives in groups. "Man," Aristotle says, "is by nature a political animal." Religion tells us what to do with our knowledge and technologies. It establishes rules of order, informs what is "right" and what is "wrong." People are not born with the values that promote culture and civilization on a high level. Ethics and morality must be deliberately inculcated. Absent moral indoctrination, people revert to their animalistic instincts.

As a skeptic, I am sympathetic with agnosticism. But I skeptical of atheism. The atheist claims there is no God. How can he be so sure? One wonders if the motivation of the average atheist is anything more than base self-interest. After all, we live in the age of entitlement. Everyone is entitled to everything, free from all the constraints imposed by religion and morality. The death of God surely makes us judges in our own cases.

Many of the arguments advanced by atheists are puerile. Most common is the invocation of the straw-man fallacy. This is the well-known intellectual fallacy wherein one distorts a proposition into an absurd straw man that is easily knocked down.

In Medieval European art, God was invariably depicted as an old man with a white beard who lives in the clouds. The most infamous example of this was painted on the ceiling of the Sistine Chapel by Michelangelo. I am not aware of any better way to portray God in a painting. But is there anyone older than three who believes that God is an elderly gentleman who lives in the clouds?

A common type of atheist is the eighteen-year-old college student who is shocked to discover what he should have figured out by the age of twelve: there is no anthropomorphic God. The eager youth, in his ignorance and vanity, immediately concludes that all conceptions of God are null and void. This, he declares to the world with the same impassioned fervor as a religious fanatic.

One is reminded of Macaulay's description of Thomas Aikenhead, the unfortunate youth who was hung for atheism in 1697. "He fancied that he had lighted upon a mine of wisdom which had been hidden from the rest of mankind, and, with the conceit from which half-educated lads of quick parts are seldom free, proclaimed his discoveries."

I might be inclined to take atheists more seriously if they exhibited any familiarity with either theology or philosophy. Since the *Dialogues* of Plato were composed in the 4th century BC, philosophers have constructed a number of classical arguments for the existence of God. These include the Cosmological Argument, the Design Argument, and the Ontological Argument. There are problems with all of these arguments. The Design Argument, for example, never really recovered from the criticisms made by David Hume in his posthumous book *Dialogues on Natural Religion* (1779). Centuries of consideration have more-or-less caused philosophers to conclude that there is no argument based on reason or observation that can do more than suggest the existence of God. As early as the eleventh century AD, the Islamic philosopher al-Ghazali (1058-1111) showed that no logical argument could prove the existence of God. Nevertheless, one might reasonably expect a professed atheist to have done their homework. But it is more commonly the case that they have never heard of the pertinent arguments, much less thought about them.

The most common argument for atheism is that there is no evidence for the existence of God. One is initially taken aback by such a striking assertion. Is it really true that there is "no" evidence for the existence of God? None? Is it not striking that theism has been nearly universal, from the dawn of recorded history throughout most if not all human civilizations? That religion has been the greatest force in human history? That religion builds and transforms human civilizations, informs culture, morality, and law? Although not impossible, it would be surprising to find that all of the preceding had been constructed on a foundation for which there is no evidence.

When an atheist asserts that there is "no evidence" for the existence of God, they mean no evidence of the type they deem acceptable. That is, scientific evidence. Evidence based on observation and reason, capable of repeated corroboration. They rather expect to find God under a microscope, or observe Heaven through a telescope, or take photographs of God when It descends from the clouds in a chariot drawn by winged horses. They demand that God supply evidence on human terms. They demand natural evidence for the supernatural.

Ants live in ant hills and underground burrows. They furiously scurry around, carrying particles of dirt, excavating tunnels and generally keeping busy on all the business that pertains to the kingdom of ants. One ant tells another of the planet Jupiter. Whereupon he is met by the indignant protest that there is no evidence for such a thing. No ant has ever observed it. The only things that exist are those things immediately perceptible to the eyes and brain of an ant. The ant, like all creatures, is unable to fathom the depths of his ignorance. It never occurs to him that his failure to perceive a thing greater than himself might originate in his own frail and limited nature. It is truly impossible to be aware of what we are not aware of. We may only hope to be cognizant that there must be much of which we are ignorant.

There is evidence for the existence of God, but it is not scientific evidence based on the epistemologies of reason and observation. The touchstone of theism is revelation. Revelation is "the disclosure or communication of knowledge by divine or supernatural means." It is the basis of religion, at least the Abrahamic faiths. When Saul was on the road to Damascus and fell off his horse, he tell us "I was taken up to heaven for a visit...and heard things so astounding that they are beyond a man's power to describe or put in words." The consequences of this incident were profound. Saul, the persecutor of the Christians, immediately converted to Christianity and became Paul, the person responsible for transforming Christianity from a Jewish sect into a new universal religion. Christianity is now the world's largest religion and the single most important historical influence on Western Civilization.

On his "night of fire" the mathematician Blaise Pascal experienced a direct apprehension of God. God, Pascal wrote, "can only be found by the ways taught in the Gospels." Saint Teresa of Avila described her ecstatic revelation as a pain "so great that it made me moan; and yet so surpassing was the sweetness of this excessive pain that I could not wish to be rid of it. The soul is satisfied with nothing less than God."

To al-Ghazali, revelation was the highest epistemology. It was above science. Knowledge of God was obtained only by "transport, ecstasy, and the transformation of the moral being." al-Ghazali concluded that when a rationalist rejects what they have not experienced, it is merely "a proof of their profound ignorance."

The atheist who demands scientific evidence for God's existence has made the same mistake as the Biblical Fundamentalist who claims the Earth is only 6000 years old. The fundamentalist applies the epistemological criterion of revelation to answer a natural question that should be addressed by scientific means.

In *Letter to the Grand Duchess Christina* (1615) Galileo explained "in the discussion of natural problems, we ought not to begin at the authority of places of scripture; but at sensible experiments and necessary demonstrations." But the question of God's existence is not a natural one. God, by definition, is supernatural. The only possible way It can be apprehended is through inspiration. To paraphrase Galileo, "in the discussion of supernatural problems, we ought not to begin with natural experiments."

The atheist who demands to stuff God in a box where It can be studied and observed has made the metaphysical assumption that only the natural world revealed to him by his senses exists. This assumption cannot be verified or tested. Science is nested within metaphysics. Like other systems of knowledge it begins with implicit assumptions. Even geometry rests upon unprovable axioms. The atheist has only asserted what needs to be demonstrated. It is no triumph to trumpet a lack of material evidence for the immaterial. Galileo summed it up nicely. "A great ineptitude exists on the part of those who would have it that God made the universe more in proportion to the small capacity of their reason than to His immense, His infinite, power."

And whence parsimony? Why do scientists still endorse Ockam's Razor? Atheistic scientists nurse a secret hypocrisy. They endorse simplicity because they implicitly hold the teleological conviction that God constructed the cosmos with beauty. Physicist Paul Dirac (1902-1984) professed "it is more important to have beauty in one's equations than to have them fit experiment."

Like folly, human vanity is inexhaustible. In *Genesis*, it is claimed that man was made in the image of God. But if God is dead, human reason has become the light of the universe. In his insufferable vanity, Man has made himself into the image of God. The roles have been reversed, but the hubris remains.

George Sarton noted that works of art provide us with "an intuitive, synthetic, and immediate knowledge" of the "deepest aspirations" of a civilization. If the death of God has illuminated our hearts and minds, why is it that our fine arts are degraded beyond recognition? Our buildings are not as beautiful as the Gothic Cathedrals of the thirteenth century. Modern painters make monochrome paintings and call them art. Are these works equal to those of the Renaissance? Are our sculptures the equal of Michelangelo's *David*? If Christian Europe before the Scientific Revolution was such a dark and ignorant age, how is it that such superlative art was made?

If God, by definition, is a spiritual principle beyond human comprehension, how can anyone be sure that It does not exist? Atheism is not only logically indefensible, but unintelligible.

47 GUN OWNERSHIP BENEFITS SOCIETY

Gun ownership is a net benefit to our society. Every year, guns in the hands of responsible citizens are used to prevent and stop crimes and save lives. How do I know? I went to the library and read the pertinent criminological literature.

In a 1995 article published in *The Journal of Criminal Law and Criminology*, professor Gary Kleck of Florida State University estimated that private citizens use guns between 2.2 and 2.5 million times each year for self-defense. Kleck is a self-described liberal Democrat and ACLU member who has never received funding from the NRA or any other gun-rights organization. His results are supported by thirteen other surveys of defensive gun use.

According to Kleck and other unbiased researchers, defensive gun uses are about three to five times more common that criminal uses. Kleck also found that about 400,000 people a year deploy firearms in situations where the act "almost certainly" saved a life. This exceeds by more than a factor of ten the number of lives lost yearly to criminal shootings.

The facts are plain and unmistakable--if the gun-grabbers are successful in disarming us, at least 400,000 innocent people will be murdered each year. In a few short years, the total number of victims may exceed the six million killed in the Nazi Holocaust.

The Second Amendment does not grant a right to "keep and bear arms" to anyone. Rather, it protects an inalienable natural right. The right exists, whether it is in the Bill of Rights or not. The Founding Fathers gave us this protection because they feared a concentration of power in the hands of a centralized government would lead to tyranny.

In *Federalist Paper No. 29*, Alexander Hamilton wrote that a standing army of the government "can never be formidable to the liberties of the people while there is a large body of citizens, little if at all inferior to them in discipline and the use of arms, who stand ready to defend their own rights and those of their fellow citizens."

In his book, *A Familiar Exposition of the Constitution of the United States*, Supreme Court Justice Joseph Story wrote "the right of the citizens to keep and bear arms...offers a strong moral check against the usurpation and arbitrary power of rulers."

There are those who claim we no longer need arms to preserve our freedom, that representative government will ensure our liberty. These people learn nothing from history. It is a historical fact that the American people earned the right to representative government through armed struggle.

In the fall of 1996, the people of Serbia voted their oppressive government out of office. That same government promptly ignored the election results and refused to relinquish power.

As the people took to the streets, fighting for freedom with snowballs, firecrackers and eggs, the government closed down independent radio stations and launched a propaganda campaign that characterized the demonstrators as "anti-government extremists."

Will this be the America of the twenty-first century?

48 MILITIAS PROTECT OUR FREEDOMS

The militia is a venerable institution in the United States. The Constitution grants Congress the power to "organize, arm and discipline" the militia, while reserving to the states the powers to "appoint the officers of the militia" and the authority to "train the militia" according to "the discipline prescribed by Congress." Notably, the Constitution also grants Congress the power to "raise and support armies" *separate* to the militia.

The Second Amendment to the Constitution speaks of the "rights of the people" in the same sentence that refers to the militia. An examination of the written record of debates concerning the ratification of the Constitution shows that the militia was understood without exception to consist of the whole body of the people. More than two-hundred years of searching have not found a single scrap of paper which supports the idea that the founders intended for the militia to be a select army under control of the US government.

Why does the Constitution provide not only for a militia but also guarantee the right of the people to keep and bear arms? The founders were *not* silent upon this question. In *Federalist Paper No. 29*, Alexander Hamilton wrote in reference to "the proper establishment of the militia."

> If circumstances should at any time oblige the government to form an army of any magnitude that army can never be formidable to the liberties of the people while there is a large body of citizens, little if at all inferior to them in discipline and the use of arms who stand ready to defend their own rights and those of their fellow citizens.

In one breathtaking sentence, Hamilton informed us of (a) who the militia consists of (the citizenry at large), (b) what type of arms the militia should possess (those enabling it to be "little if at all inferior" to the regular army, and (c) the primary purpose of the militia (to guard against government tyranny.)

The militia is meant to be part of the checks and balances in our system of government; it is the ultimate safeguard against tyranny. For the first time in the long history of the United States, mlitia groups are now spontaneously organizing throughout the country.

Should not the perceptive among us question as to why this should be so? Should we not also wonder why Congress has abdicated its responsibility to "organize, arm and discipline" the militia but has also attempted to destroy the militia by taking away the right of the people to keep and bear arms?

If the militia groups that have formed do not constitute a well-regulated militia, who is to blame? What choice do the people have when the US government not only abandons its responsibilities but exceeds its lawful authority under the Constitution?

In these difficult and tumultuous times are we to trust our civil liberties and freedom to the empty rhetoric of politicians and the professional soldiers in their employ? Or should we be more disposed to trust the militia--a body composed of our friends, neighbors and relatives, whose only interests are to preserve and protect our common freedom?

49 NEVER GIVE UP YOUR WEAPONS

History demonstrates that destruction awaits those who attempt to placate their enemies by surrendering their weapons. In 149 BC, half a million citizens of Carthage tried to appease Rome by turning over their armaments. But instead of buying peace they only facilitated their own destruction. Ninety percent of the Carthaginians were killed and the city of Carthage was razed to the ground. Those who survived were sold into slavery, and Carthaginian civilization was forever wiped from the face of the earth.

The story of how the Carthaginians sealed their fate by delivering their weapons into the hands of their enemy is fully chronicled in my book, *Science and Technology in World History, Volume 1: The Ancient World and Classical Civilization.*

Carthage was founded on the shores of North Africa by Phoenicians in the 9th century BC. It was the center of a powerful and ancient empire, and as the power of Rome grew, it was inevitable that the Romans and Carthaginians would come into conflict.

Between 264 and 146 BC, Rome and Carthage fought three Punic Wars for control of the Mediterranean. The Romans were victorious in both the First and Second Punic Wars. At the close of the Second Punic War in 202 BC, Carthage was forced to pay Rome 200 talents of silver a year for fifty years. An additional term of peace was that Carthage was forbidden from waging war without Rome's permission. Consequently, Numidians in North Africa began to raid Carthage without fear of reprisal. When the Carthaginians begged Rome for permission to defend themselves, they were refused.

In 157 BC, Cato the Censor visited Carthage and was alarmed to discover how quickly the Carthaginians had recovered from their defeat in the Second Punic War. He acquired the conviction that Rome would never be secure until Carthage was completely annihilated. Cato began to close every speech in the Roman Senate by exclaiming, "Carthage must be destroyed!"

As time passed, the Roman Senate became convinced that Cato was right and resolved to wipe Carthage off the face of the earth. But they needed a pretext for commencing hostilities. The Carthaginians unwittingly supplied one.

Under the terms of peace that had concluded the Second Punic War, Carthage had been required to pay tribute to Rome for fifty years. When the fifty years had passed, the Carthaginians reasoned that they were also free from the restriction that forbade them from waging war without the permission of Rome. A patriotic faction came to power in Carthage and formed an army to defend Carthage from the Numidian raids.

The war between the Carthaginians and Numidians provided Rome with the pretext it needed, and the Roman Senate promptly declared war on Carthage. When the Carthaginians learned that a state of war existed, they became alarmed and immediately dispatched a team of thirty ambassadors to Rome to plead for peace. Carthage was in no condition to fight a Third Punic War with Rome. Since its victory in the Second Punic War, Rome had grown immeasurably more powerful.

The Roman Senate had already resolved on the destruction of Carthage, but they reasoned it would be advantageous to first employ treachery. So they dealt with the Carthaginians in a way that was both brutal and deceitful.

The Carthaginian ambassadors were told that their desire for peace would be granted. Carthage would be allowed to retain its freedom, territory, and property. But as a condition and guarantee of peace, the Carthaginians were required to surrender three hundred male children from their most eminent families as hostages. Roman military forces were dispatched to Carthage to collect the captives. The commanding Roman consuls were secretly instructed to wage war until Carthage was "razed to the ground."

According to the historian Appian (c. AD 95-165), the Carthaginian children had to be ripped from the arms of their mothers. Some of the mothers were so distraught that they tore out their hair, beat on their breasts, or even swam out to sea, vainly following the ships carrying their sons off to Rome. They would never see their children alive again. But this sacrifice was judged necessary to purchase peace.

Once the hostages had been surrendered, the Carthaginian ambassadors expected peace. But the Romans had a new demand. They insisted that the Carthaginians surrender their weapons--all of them. The Roman Consul Censorinus explained, "if you are sincerely desirous of peace, why do you need any arms?" He continued, "bring all your weapons and engines of war, both public and private, and deliver them to us."

Oblivious to the Roman maxim, "if you want peace, prepare for war," the Carthaginians obsequiously complied. They turned over armor for 200,000 men, javelins, darts, and 2,000 catapults. Appian said that it was an "unparalleled spectacle to behold the vast number of loaded wagons."

Having complied with the Roman request to surrender their weapons, the Carthaginian ambassadors foolishly thought they had bought peace by disarming themselves. The consul Censorinus praised the Carthaginians for having the wisdom to comply with the Roman's first two requirements. But there was yet another new demand. "Yield Carthage to us, and betake yourselves where you like within your own territory at a distance of at least ten miles from the sea, for we are resolved to raze your city to the ground."

The Carthaginian ambassadors finally realized they had been deceived into yielding to Rome, without a fight, everything it could have expected from waging and winning another war. There would be no peace, and they had been artfully deceived. The Carthaginian ambassadors "cursed the Romans...flung themselves to the ground and beat it with their hands and heads. Some of them even tore their clothes and lacerated their flesh as though they were absolutely bereft of their senses."

Having surrendered their swords, the Carthaginians could only resort to words. So they appealed to the Romans for mercy and pity. But none was granted. The consul Censorinus stated "the Senate...has issued its decrees and they must be carried out." He explained, "we do not make this decision from any ill-will toward you, but in the interest of a lasting peace and of the common security." The only consolation the Roman consul could offer to the Carthaginians was the observation that "the healing drug for all evils is oblivion."

When the Carthaginian ambassadors brought the fateful news back to Carthage, there followed "a scene of blind, raving madness." Some people fell upon the ambassadors and ripped them to pieces or stoned them to death. The Carthaginians went into their armories, and collapsed, sobbing, when they found them empty. Most distraught of all were the mothers who had surrendered their children to the Romans. It was now apparent that the loss of their offspring had accomplished no good whatsoever.

The Carthaginians had been disarmed, but nevertheless resolved to resist as much as possible. They worked day and night to forge new weapons. Statues were melted down for their metal. Women cut off their hair to provide strings for catapults. Assisting the belated resistance was Carthage's immensely strong fortifications. Most of the city was surrounded by a series of three walls, each forty-five feet high. The walls had been reinforced for centuries. It was the strength of these fortifications that had dissuaded the Romans from attempting the destruction of Carthage at the end of the Second Punic War.

The outcome was predetermined from the beginning, but the Romans were forced to resort to a long siege to finally subdue Carthage. To cut off the Carthaginian supply routes by sea, large engineering works had to be constructed, and this took time.

After three years, the Carthaginians were weakened by hunger and disease and the Romans finally managed to breach the city walls. There followed six days of fighting, street-by-street, but the Carthaginian resistance was feeble.

The city was set on fire, and there followed endless scenes of horror as the fires consumed both buildings and people. The Romans killed everyone that resisted. The survivors, totaling 55,000, represented less than ten percent of the original population. They were sold into slavery. The Roman Senate decreed that what remained of Carthage be utterly destroyed. The ruins burned for seventeen days. Seven hundred years of Carthaginian civilization came to a bitter end.

Thus the lesson was learned. Surrendering your weapons does not buy peace, but only paves the way for ultimate defeat. If you want peace, prepare for war.

50 THE BILL OF RIGHTS HAS BEEN EVISCERATED

I much prefer the original and complete version of the Bill of Rights to the revisionist and redacted version advocated by the politically correct. However, I also understand why the complete Bill of Rights cannot be celebrated today.

According to leftists, our rights as Americans come from our Constitution. This is not what the authors of the Constitution and the Bill of Rights understood. The Founding Fathers believed that our rights come from God, and they wrote the Constitution and Bill of Rights to protect these natural rights.

Nowhere in the Bill of Rights will you find a statement to the effect that "the people shall have the right." Rather, the text of the Bill of Rights enjoins the government of the United States from infringing on rights that predate and supersede it.

The entire philosophy of our unique form of government was stated succinctly by Thomas Jefferson in the Declaration of Independence. Jefferson introduced the Declaration by noting "men...are endowed by their Creator with certain unalienable rights" and "governments are instituted among men...to secure these rights."

I supposed none of us are going to get very excited about the neglect of the Third Amendment which protects us from the government quartering troops in our homes without our permission. However the Second, Ninth, and Tenth Amendments are now neglected and ignored.

The Second Amendment states that a well-regulated militia is necessary to the security of a free state, and therefore the right of the people to keep and bear arms shall not be infringed. Because guns are now politically incorrect, the Second Amendment has become something of an embarrassment.

So we are told that the "right of the people" is really "the right of the government." This would have been very surprising to George Mason, the Virginian who was the driving force behind the adoption of the Bill of Rights. Mason asked, "what is the militia? It is the whole people, except for a few public officials." Mason also warned that "to disarm the people is the best and most effectual way to enslave them."

The Ninth Amendment stipulates that the enumeration of certain rights in the Constitution shall not be construed to deny or disparage other rights retained by the people. What rights? Maybe the right to travel freely, the right to buy, possess, and use drugs and medicines, and the right to work without being enrolled as a numbered drone in the social security system. These and many other rights enjoyed by our forefathers and guaranteed by our Constitution have been lost.

Finally we arrive at the Tenth Amendment. It states that the powers not delegated to the United States by the Constitution are reserved to the States or to the people. The Tenth Amendment implies that all powers originate in the people and that we have delegated only a few and specific powers to the United States.

The powers granted to Congress are enumerated in Article 1, Section 8 of the Constitution. By and large, the people of the United States have no idea what is in Article 1, Section 8. If they read it, they might be surprised to find that they never delegated any power to Congress to create a welfare or social security system, interfere in our schools, ban guns, regulate medicines and drugs, outlaw incandescent light bulbs, or mandate water-saving toilets.

In fact, there is nothing in the Constitution that authorizes ninety percent or more of what the government of the United States does.

Although I much prefer the original and complete Bill of Rights, it is now little more than history. It is entirely proper to cut out half of the Bill of Rights, because fully half or more of our freedoms and rights have been lost.

51 COMMODITIES AND SERVICES ARE NOT RIGHTS

Commodities and services are not rights. The advocates of welfare rights are fond of describing in glowing terms how a compassionate, civilized society provides such items as an education or health care to its citizens. But they seldom address the question of who is to pay for these commodities, how payment is to be extracted (by force), or what is to be done with those who refuse to provide the items they claim as rights (presumably those who resist will be imprisoned or killed).

We must confront the reality that if health care and education are truly rights, not privileges, they *must* be provided, regardless of the willingness of teachers, doctors, or nurses to comply. Simply put, the "compassionate and civilized" society that the advocates of welfare rights promote is based on slavery.

As a rational being I cannot conceive of "rights" for some that are purchased at the cost of enslaving others. I therefore reject the concept of welfare rights as a moral abomination.

The legislative body of the government of the United States, the Congress, cannot legally do whatever it wants unless it exercises one of the few and specific powers granted to it by the Constitution.

I suggest to readers that they obtain a copy of the Constitution and read it for themselves. The Constitution was written by and for the people, not lawyers, judges, or a self-appointed pseudo-intellectual elite.

Those who do read this document will find that the limited powers of Congress are enumerated in Article 1, Section 8, just as I have asserted. Just because the existing body of professional politicians have greatly exceeded their legal authority through the complicity of a derelict judiciary is no justification for further incursions on our liberties.

I have offered the countries of Cuba and the Soviet Union as examples of archetypical welfare states. My critics prefer the socialist, but democratic societies of western Europe. I chose Cuba and the Soviet Union simply because they represent more nearly pure socialist systems than countries such as France, Germany, or England, and therefore make my point more clearly.

In Cuba there is no legal private ownership of land or private businesses. In the democracies of western Europe, the forceful expropriation of private property by the state is partial, not total. An individual may own land or a business, but is subject to heavy taxes and regulation.

Western European states which have mixed economies are not sustained by the socialist elements of their systems. Rather, it is the capitalist elements which sustain the burden of the welfare states and allow them to keep their heads above water. If socialism was sustaining the mixed economic systems of western Europe, then it logically follows that pure socialist states such as Cuba would be utopias, while the more nearly pure capitalist systems found in the United States and Hong Kong would have produced misery and poverty.

In summary, I believe in both the moral and pragmatic superiority of freedom: there is no other choice. Karl Popper explained why he rejected socialism.

> If there could be such a thing as socialism combined with individual liberty, I would be a socialist still. For nothing could be better than living a modest, simple, and free life in an egalitarian society. It took some time before I recognized this as no more than a beautiful dream; that freedom is more important that equality; that the attempt to realize equality endangers freedom; and that, if freedom is lost, there will not even be equality among the unfree.

ABOUT THE AUTHOR

David Deming (b. 1954) is associate professor of Arts and Sciences at the University of Oklahoma in Norman. He graduated from Indiana University in 1983 with a BS degree in geology, and received a Ph.D in geophysics from the University of Utah in 1988. Prior to his arrival at the University of Oklahoma in 1992, Deming held a National Research Council postdoctoral fellowship at the US Geological Survey in California. From 1992 through 2005, Dr. Deming was an assistant and associate professor in the School of Geology and Geophysics at the University of Oklahoma. Deming is an adjunct faculty member at the *Oklahoma Council of Public Affairs* and the *National Center for Policy Analysis*. Dr. Deming has contributed more than forty peer-reviewed research papers to the scientific literature. He is the author of a textbook on hydrogeology, *Introduction to Hydrogeology* (2002), and a trilogy on the history of science, *Science and Technology in World History, Volumes 1, 2, and 3*.

Made in the USA
Lexington, KY
02 March 2013